HORST

INTERIORS

HORST

INTERIORS

by BARBARA PLUMB

A Bulfinch Press Book
Little, Brown and Company
BOSTON • NEW YORK • TORONTO • LONDON

For my son, Christian

With thanks to dear Nicholas Lawford for his early support and help, and to Rick Tardiff, who takes such wonderful care of Horst and his photographs. Also, I want to express my gratitude to Bill Rayner, editorial business manager at Condé Nast, for his cooperation, assistance, and good suggestions; and to the wonderful threesome in the Condé Nast library, Cindy Cathcart, Fred Keith, and Don Osterweil, who know everything and can find out anything; and to Barbara Hackney, the head of Condé Nast's photo reproduction department. Particular thanks go to Mary Gilliatt for her valuable and valued second opinions. Designer Timothy Shaner has been fabulous to work with, not only because of his creative flair, but also because of his help with photo research and editing. I would especially like to thank the terrific team at Welcome—Lena Tabori, Hiro Clark, Ellen Mendlow, and Jonathan Glick—for their dedication to quality and hard work. Thanks go as well to the much-missed Markus Frey and Nan Wise. I would also like to express deep appreciation to Ray Roberts, my distinguished editor, who believed in this project from the start, and to Carol Judy Leslie, publisher of Bulfinch, who was born a Horst fan. Special thanks, also, to Marisa Bartolucci, for her wise suggestions and astute editing. Finally, I would like to thank Nancy Evans for her wisdom and moral support.—*Barbara Plumb*

Special acknowledgment is made to The Condé Nast Publications Inc. for its cooperation and assistance with the research and reproduction of the images in this volume.

Book design by Timothy Shaner
Produced by Welcome Enterprises, Inc., New York

First Edition

ISBN 0-8212-2046-2

Library of Congress Catalog Card Number 93-77592

Bulfinch Press is an imprint and trademark of Little, Brown and Company (Inc.)
Published simultaneously in Canada by Little, Brown & Company (Canada) Limited

PRINTED IN JAPAN

CONTENTS

Horst by Duane Michals (1984).

PREFACE

The interiors photography that Horst did, most particularly for *Vogue* but also for *House & Garden*, in the 1960s, 1970s, and 1980s was remarkable for many reasons. First, as design history, this body of work represents the most important record of how a special breed of the rich and famous—those with the most sophisticated taste and highest style—lived. Second, as a history of design, it is a marvelous limning of the changes in trends and ideas over three important decades during which a mini design revolution came and went. Looking at the interiors decade by decade, there is no mistaking which are the here-today, gone-tomorrow caprices and which, the overarching classic ideals of beauty that supersede style, period, and nationality.

A dividend accompanies each of the interiors by Horst: at least one unforgettable portrait of the person in residence. These portraits are not the posed and stiff icons seen all too frequently in high-style magazines, but relaxed, easy distillations of the particular personality of the subject. Without the glory of the splendid interior decoration accompanying them, these portraits would still stand on their own. Writers, fashion designers, artists, industrialists, arrivistes, celebrities-for-a-minute, aristocrats—the photographer captured a fascinating array of characters who lived in a unique collection of rooms.

Horst's entrée to the most remarkable houses and apartments resulted from a combination of factors: the elitist prestige of *Vogue* and *House & Garden,* his reputation for making everything and everyone look beautiful—or at least interesting—and a desire for publicity among the so-called right people.

This confluence of great houses, great people, and a great photographer is unlikely ever to occur again. At the end of the 1980s the monied and powerful began to lower their profile, worrying about being robbed or kidnapped—or revealing too much to the tax man. Thus, Horst leaves us with a visual history of interior design that is unique. Through his timeless photographs, we can enjoy houses of extraordinary splendor, luxury, and art, as well as those exuding flair, imagination, and the force of personality.

NOTE: I have written about the interiors and those who lived in them *historically,* that is, places and people are "freeze framed" in the decades when Horst actually photographed them. No update is given on which individuals have subsequently died or disappeared, or which couples have separated, divorced, or been widowed. This back-to-the-future approach replays—in both pictures and text—the idealized world that Horst walked into, recorded, and forever preserved.

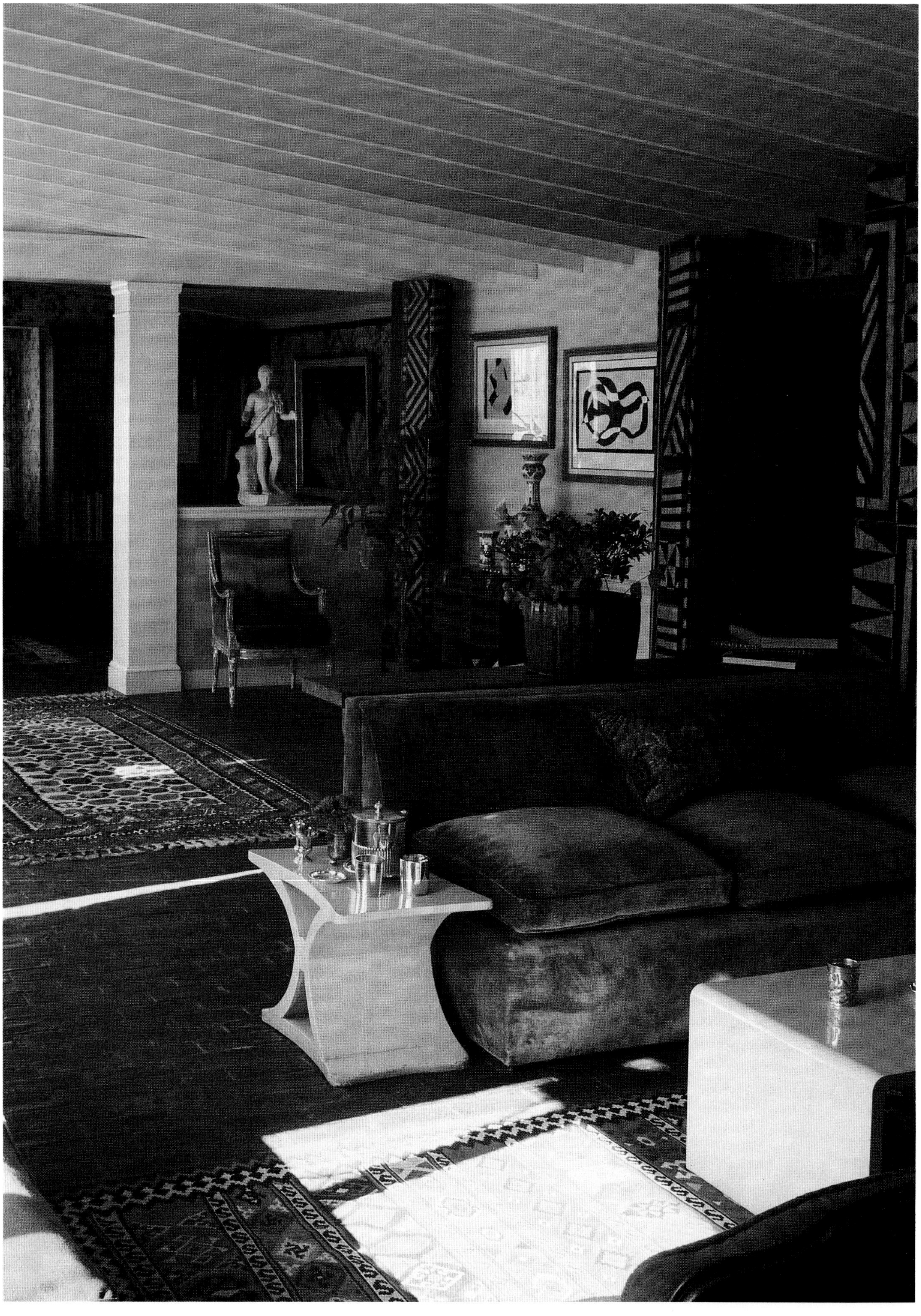

Horst's living room in Oyster Bay, Long Island, features a Louis XVI chair with needlepoint by Horst himself, a table by Jean-Michel Frank, and a screen made of tapa cloth given to Horst by Chanel (1966).

INTRODUCTION

I came to know Horst during my thirteen years as "Living" editor at *Vogue*. At that time I frequently went on assignments with him both in the United States and in Europe. From the beginning, I was impressed by his natural artistic talent and his zeal for hard work. But, above all, what seemed to empower Horst were his enormous personal charm and stunning good looks.

The first time I worked with him, as he photographed the model rooms in the newly completed Olympic Tower condominium in New York, I immediately fell for his big grin, his cigarette-husky bass voice, his wicked gray-blue eyes, his exuberant good humor, and his gift for storytelling. During photography shoots he would regale me and his assistant with remarkable tales about his famous friends: Coco Chanel, Greta Garbo, Noël Coward, Truman Capote, Consuelo Balsan, Elsa Schiaparelli, Luchino Visconti. The list seemed endless.

Horst and Chanel were soul mates. Both outsiders, they were self-made sophisticates—Chanel, a young girl from the French countryside, and Horst, the son of a burgher from a town in the Thuringia area of eastern Germany. Horst appreciated Chanel's gutsiness. "She pretended to be the Queen of Paris. She made her own taste and the world's taste," he would say. "She didn't like society, not French society, but they liked her."

However, she did like Horst—from the start. "The first time I visited her apartment at the Ritz," he once told me, "I saw a huge baroque angel, and said: 'Isn't it wonderful?' The next day I had it." He still seemed startled by her generosity decades later.

Horst was also friendly with a style setter of a later age, the legendary Pauline Fairfax Potter, who was to become the wife of Baron Philippe de Rothschild. The photographer remembered first meeting her in New York—when she was still unmarried and working for Hattie Carnegie. They met at a cocktail party, where, he recalled, Miss Potter struck an unusual pose. "She was a tall girl, and she sat on a low chair," Horst recounted, "with her long legs spread wide apart. I had never seen a lady sitting in such a way. I said, 'You'd better come and be photographed.' She did, and I photographed her just like that."

Whomever Horst photographed he beguiled. It was magic to watch him at portrait sittings. To relax his subjects he would start off chatting, joking, and spinning tall tales. When the rapport had jelled, he would ask for a Dubonnet or a Campari, depending on his mood, and then start clicking away with his Rolleiflex or Hasselblad. Even the stiffest and most fidgety of subjects overcame any natural shyness and fear of the camera in Horst's presence because he made each one feel appreciated and beautiful. The whole process was so much like a seduction that often other people in the room felt like intruders—or voyeurs.

When he went on assignment to photograph a great house somewhere abroad, he would inevitably stay for a couple of weeks. He liked to have a stretch of days so he could see what light most flattered each room. "I always waited for the best light—six in the morning, eight, twelve," Horst remembers. "Sometimes it would be better in the afternoon. It depended. I looked at it several times in the day." Even after he had gotten all the shots he wanted, his hosts were reluctant to let him go because he was such an entertaining house guest.

The natural lighting Horst chose for his interiors photography was the opposite of the dramatic, high-contrast sculptural lighting with which he had made his reputation as a fashion photographer. When photographing rooms, he preferred minimal artificial light to illuminate dark corners and preserve natural shadows. When photographing Château de Mouton, the Rothschild's house in the southwest of France, for example, he relied solely on the daylight that streamed in through the windows.

When Horst did add supplementary lighting, he chose tungsten spotlights over strobes, the preferred lighting of so many other photographers. "You have to see what you are photographing, and with strobes you don't," he explains.

If Horst had achieved drama in his fashion photography by using high-contrast lighting, he achieved it in his interiors by focusing on details. And juxtapositions. And layerings of textures and colors into rich, sensual, painterly compositions. All are quintessential Horst.

The cover photograph of this book, showing the embroidered slipper of Baron Philippe de Rothschild resting on a carpet portrait of Napoleon III, epitomizes Horst's genius for evocative detail. It has been said that you can tell everything about a person by what they have on their bedside table. Horst understood that. He liked to get in close, showing what people collect, what objects they treasure. To him, it is not the whole room that reveals taste as much as it is the little unexpected details.

Horst's unusual juxtapositions never cease to delight, such as the table holding a star burst ornament that appears to emblazon Paloma Picasso's dress as she stands nearby in her New York apartment, or a still life of silver brushes against Chinese wallpaper at Baron Rothschild's Château de Mouton, or the illusion of motion in a blackamoor, which seems to be dancing, at the Italian weekend villa of Marella and Giovanni Agnelli.

Of the many interiors Horst has photographed on assignment, his personal favorite is "The Cottage," which is owned by David Somerset. "I loved the way everything was pulled together. It

The apartment of Horst and Baron George von Hoyningen-Huene on the rue St. Romain in Paris (1931).

was extraordinary," Horst recalls. "These people still live exactly as they used to in the seventeenth century."

Horst's interiors portraits—just a bit off, slightly unexpected—always pulsate with vibrancy and life. "I think of the people first, how they will photograph," he says. "I try to consider what they can do in the house, and try to place them where they will be happy. Maybe it's interesting architecturally or the color is right, but I don't think about the interiors, just the person. With certain people it's much better to have them stand out, red against black, or whatever. With others it's much easier to blend them in with the background."

~

One of the reasons Horst is such a sensitive photographer of houses and interiors is that he has been keenly interested in architecture and decoration since he was a boy. Born in Germany in 1906, the second son of a hardware store owner, he was christened Horst Paul Albert Bohrmann, but changed his name to Horst P. Horst during World War II because he shared his surname with Martin Bormann, one of Hitler's chief advisers. Horst lived in Weissenfels-an-der-Saale, in a substantial bourgeois house built in 1450. (In 1992, after decades of living abroad, he received Das Grosse Verdienstkreuz, an accolade comparable to France's Order of the Legion of Honor.) His mother decorated the house in the Biedermeier style, giving a prominent place to her collection of Meissen ware and to needlepoint cushions. "Her needlepoints were some of the most beautiful I have ever seen," says Horst.

As a teenager, Horst socialized with students from the Bauhaus, the vanguard school of art, design, and architecture in Weimar, and he went to study applied art at the Kunstgewerbeschule in Hamburg in order to work with Walter Gropius, the founder of the Bauhaus and a leading modernist architect.

In 1930 Le Corbusier offered Horst an unpaid internship in his Paris atelier. Eager for the opportunity to work with the renowned architect and to enjoy the high life of Paris, he jumped at the chance. Soon after he started, however, he became disillusioned with Le Corbusier's architecture. "Much as I admired his innovative genius," Horst recalls, "the workers' dwellings he was designing at the time seemed more to me like prison cells than livable apartments."

Around the time Horst exited Le Corbusier's employ, quite by chance he had the great good fortune to meet at a café Baron George von Hoyningen-Huene, the premier fashion photographer for French *Vogue*. Hoyningen-Huene befriended Horst (who was six years his junior) both professionally and personally, making him his protégé, assistant, student of life, sometime model, and full-time apartment mate. A temperamental Baltic aristocrat whose father had run Czar Nicholas II's stables, Hoyningen-Huene introduced Horst to the worldly emigré circle of White Russians and to the great artistic, intellectual, and fashion personalities of the day: Pablo Picasso, Jean Cocteau, Gertrude

Stein, Salvador Dalí, Christian (Bébé) Bérard, Misia Sert, and Jean-Michel Frank. Horst was, in fact, one of the first to collect the classically simple furnishings, crafted out of the most luxurious materials, that his friend Jean-Michel Frank designed.

Having a collection of friends such as these at such a formative time of his life prepared Horst to meet his illustrious sitters on equal ground. When it came to sophistication and refinement, no one intimidated Horst. Rather than having to entreat people to pose for him, most—women especially—were only too eager to be photographed by him, for he had quickly earned a reputation for making his subjects look beautiful—sometimes even more beautiful than they thought they deserved.

~

Horst came to interiors in the early 1960s, when style changes in fashion photography were precipitating a dip in his career. The look shifted from stylized black-and-white studio shots, on which Horst had built his reputation, to realistic location shots featuring models in motion and in color. As often happens with adversity, it was the closing of one door that opened another.

The idea came from Diana Vreeland, soon to be editor in chief of *Vogue*. Inspired by a photograph Horst had taken of Madame Consuelo Balsan sitting in her spacious living room, she decided it would be a wonderful idea to assign Horst to photograph well-known socialites, rising celebrities, and important artists in their houses. She commissioned Valentine Lawford (a.k.a. Nicholas), a former diplomat, painter, author, and four-star charmer as the writer for this new "Fashions in Living" feature. What enhanced the arrangement was that Lawford and Horst had lived together for fifteen years.

The subject of their first assignment was their friend Consuelo Balsan, an American who had once been the Duchess of Marlborough. "She lived on Long Island in a leftover eighteenth-century elegance," Horst vividly recalls. "Like certain Americans, she wanted to appear European. Her house looked more French than any of the French houses I have ever photographed."

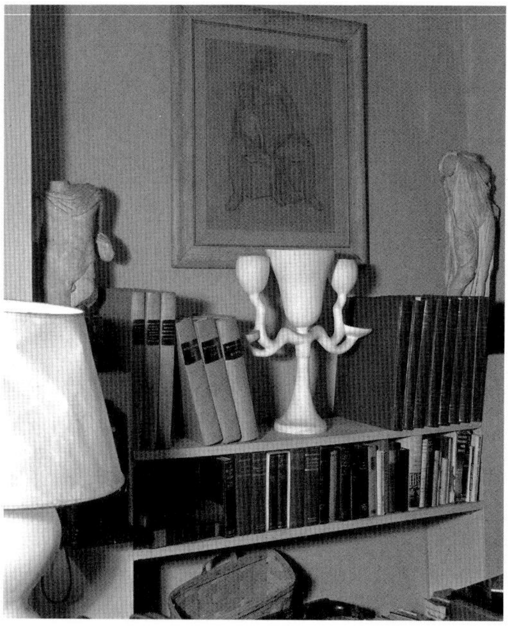

In the study of his Sutton Place apartment, Horst displayed his Picasso gouache and his vase and lamp by Diego Giacometti (1939).

Horst has emphatic ideas about what he likes in his own interiors. "Nothing that's showy," he says. "In general, I like all white for the main rooms. My kitchen and bathroom are blue-and-white and the guest room is Meissen blue. I like a mixture of modern furnishings and antiques. Certainly not *all* antiques in a new country like America. That's not right. They belong to Europe."

Horst designed and built a modern house for himself on seven acres of the former Tiffany estate in Oyster Bay, Long Island. He bought the property in 1945, soon after he was discharged from the United States Army, in which he had served as a photographer. Later, he bought another five acres with the proceeds from the sale of a favorite Picasso, *Red Clown and Blue Boy*, which had been given to him by a friend as repayment for a $5,000 loan.

"I just wanted a simple, little one-story house," Horst says. "White, not pretentious, not ostentatious, just comfortable." He remembers how some of his European friends, used to more luxurious surroundings, would quip: "Why do you want to live in a chicken coop?"

A vignette of an iris in papier-maché and a photostat of a Horst photograph of a statue in Rome (composed in Horst's Manhattan studio/pied-à-terre, about 1957).

The building, which has diverse design roots in the Bauhaus, Tunisian architecture, American ranch houses, and Provençal villas, is spare and relaxed in feeling, though the gardens are quite formal, with five radiating *allées*. The center *allée* is lined with two magnificent copper beech trees, yews, and hemlocks, which Horst and Lawford planted and shaped themselves. Horst recalls that when they planted the trees, their friends teased them because they were only a foot tall.

The house is filled with the treasures of a lifetime—portraits by Bérard of Horst and of Chanel; watercolors by Dalí; lithographs by Braque; favorite photographs by Horst of Jacqueline Onassis and Katharine Hepburn; drawings by Cocteau; botanicals by Nicholas Lawford; lamps and vases by Diego Giacometti; chairs, tables, desks, and bookcases by Jean-Michel Frank; Greek fragments; and needlepoint pillows by Horst and his mother. Every object has a personal story. Pointing to a screen made out of Polynesian tapa cloth, Horst says: "Chanel gave it to me. She didn't know what to do with it. And I didn't know what to do with it either, so I cut it up to make screens."

To see Horst's house is to know what interior design should be about—personal style and easy comfort. Whenever asked whether his own house is his favorite, he flashes his roguish smile and bellows: "And how!"—the quintessential Horst expletive.

This book is a salute to Horst, the greatest interiors photographer of our time, and possibly of any to come. And how!

Barbara Plumb
New York, New York

CONSUELO BALSAN

1963

Imagine, at the age of eighty, the optimism and energy—to say nothing of the wealth—required to buy and renovate a large but not-yet-grand house and transform it into an American palace. That is what Consuelo Vanderbilt Balsan did with her beloved "Garden Side" in Southampton, Long Island. In this long drawing room, which she added to the house, Madame Balsan conjured the blithe spirit of a sun room, rather than the heaviness of a regal retreat, by installing long windows, draping them with yellow silk, and scattering a shimmer of reflective surfaces. She positioned Louis XV furniture, which she admires for its comfort as well as its elegance, in an airy arrangement around the room's perimeter. A crystal chandelier by Baguès overhangs a spectacular Savonnerie rug that presents a précis of all the colors in the room.

~ above ~

Charmingly painted panels—pockets of paradise each—give this rococo reception room its name: *salone dipinto* (painted room). Seventeenth-century Neopolitan gilt-and-bronze blackamoors take on life, as if in eternal dance, atop a Piedmontese console.

A ravishing bouquet of pink and yellow roses from the garden, in a simple glass bowl, enhances the luncheon table. Plain white mats and napkins focus full attention on the elegant china, glassware, and flowers.

A Chinese dish with crackers, a glass of water, and a white napkin cool down the exuberance of a little-patterned tray table on a large-patterned Aubusson rug.

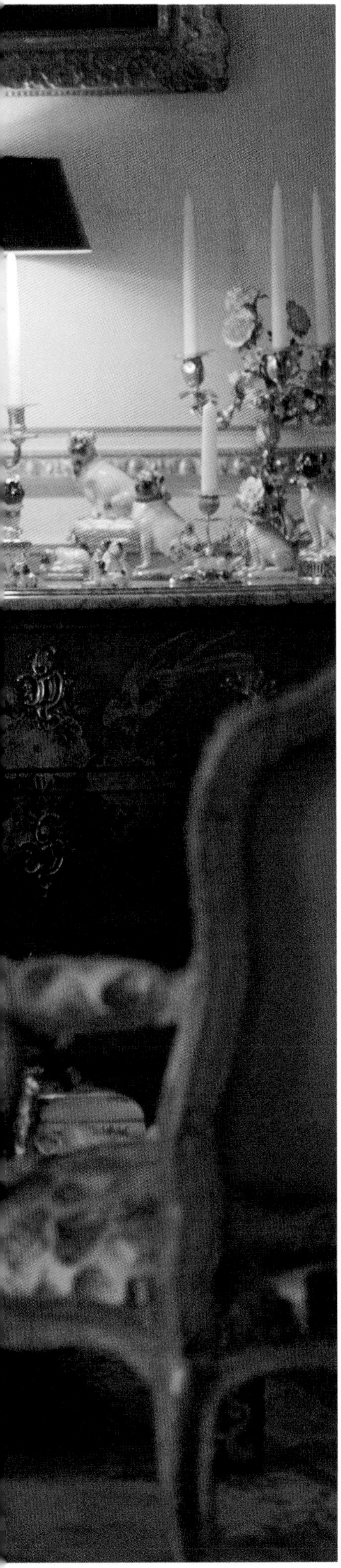

DUKE & DUCHESS OF WINDSOR

1964

The Duke and Duchess of Windsor have created a palace of their own just across the English Channel, in Paris. When they are not traveling, sojourning in New York, or sunning on the Costa del Sol, they headquarter in this slate-roofed, stone-faced mini-Trianon. It sits in a private park in the Bois de Boulogne and is leased to them by the City of Paris. The favored afternoon sport of the duchess is scouring the *antiquaires* on the Left Bank for rare eighteenth-century French furniture. Luxury, beauty, efficiency, and style are what her life is about. Her splendid surroundings begin with majestic spaces and richly paneled walls, and end with exquisite bibelots and objects in vermeil, porcelain, enamel, and gold. No detail passes her notice or interest. She even designed the dining room chairs to meet her rigorous standard of comfort. The duke and duchess sit in the living room amid their beloved pugs, their pets at their feet and their Meissen miniature dogs arrayed behind.

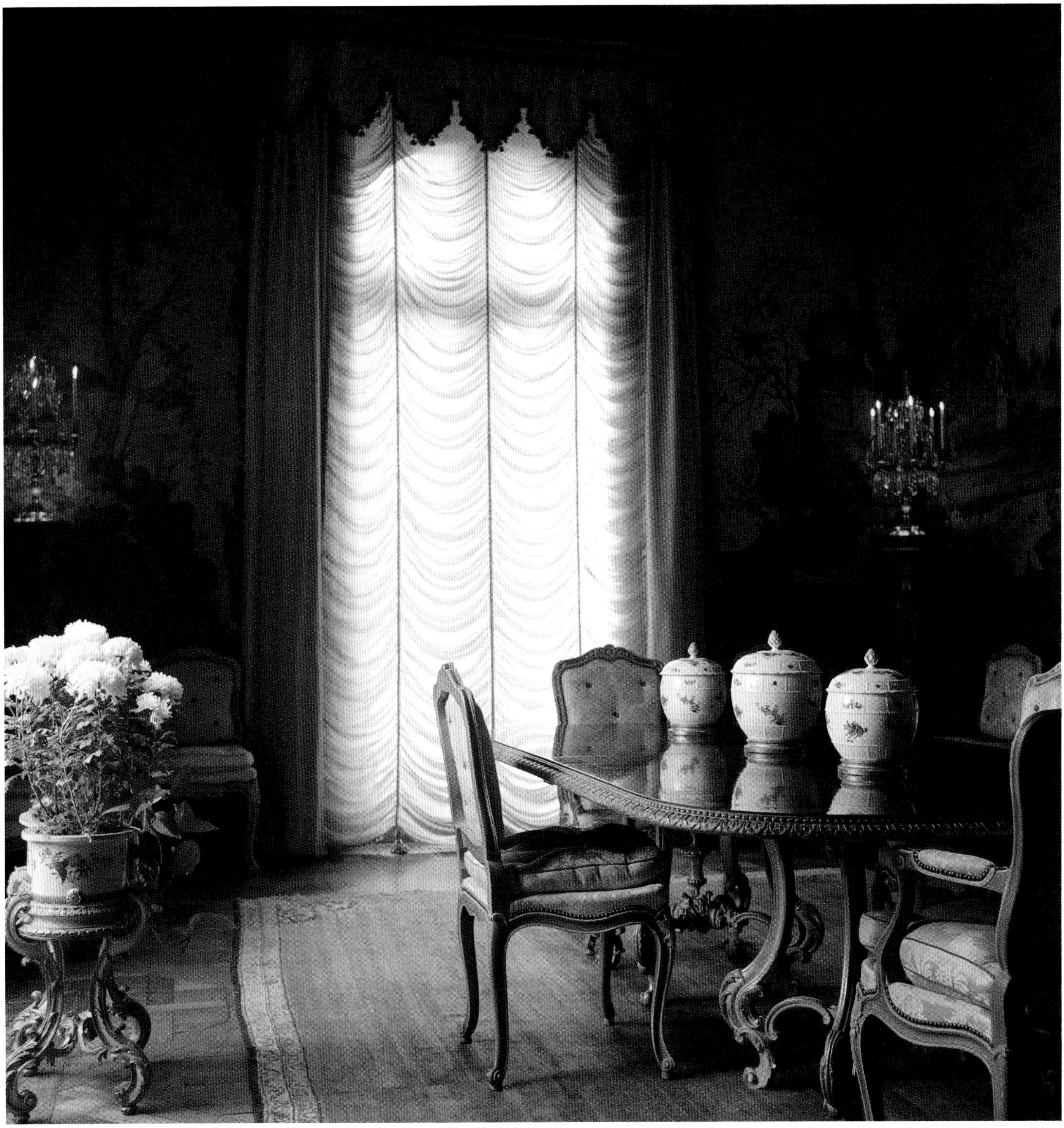

~ above ~

French chinoiserie wallpaper panels key the soft, coral pink color scheme of the graceful dining room. Painted blue-green chairs with tufted white damask seats and backs were designed by the duchess. Meissen porcelain jars from the Windsor's "Flying Tiger" dinner service ornament the table.

~ above left ~

In the entrance hall Mr. Disraeli, Mr. Chu, Davy Crockett, Trooper, and Imp—the Windsor pugs— are corralled on a Bessarabian rug by the duke's valet, who is dressed in scarlet-and-gold evening livery. Their magnificent surroundings include a superb eighteenth-century English console with a gilded, spread-eagle base and a Louis XIII chair.

~ below left ~

Painted by Sir James Gunn, a full-length portrait of the duke in the robes of the Order of the Garter hangs in the drawing room. Pale blue walls are outlined with silver-tasseled moldings.

TRUMAN CAPOTE

1965

When Truman Capote goes to Long Island, it is not to relax by the ocean—but to work within sight of it. He gutted a small, plain wooden house with the express purpose of creating a get-away-from-them-all writing studio. Not one guest room was included in his plan. What he designed for himself was a double-height living room with books upstairs and down. In addition to favoring bright colors in his wardrobe, Mr. Capote likes to decorate with them. Wherever possible, he lavished rich, jewel-like hues, inspired by the shade of his Tiffany lamp, on chairs, stools, and pillows, and he painted the floor a brilliant blue. His collecting instincts are decidedly eclectic: a brass trivet emblazoned with "Home Sweet Home," a wild boar sculpture, a stag's head, an owl vase, glass paperweights, and photographs of his friends. Andy Warhol's 1955 portrait of Mr. Capote leans against a white-painted brick fireplace.

OBSERVA
-TIONS
RICHARD
AVEDON

BARONESS PAULINE DE ROTHSCHILD

1963~1969

In the early 1950s a young American from Baltimore, Pauline Fairfax Potter, came to Paris to audition for the role of expatriate. In the course of putting down roots, she became infatuated with a charming four-room apartment-cum-garden located in the "wrong" part of town. She found the apartment, remodeled it, and infatuation became love. Even after her marriage to Baron Philippe de Rothschild in 1954, she decided to stay put. (He did too, in larger, more lavish quarters on a grand, haute-bourgeois Paris avenue.) The twain meet five months a year at Baron Philippe's famous wine-making Château de Mouton in the Médoc. As she enters her Paris bedroom, the baroness exults in a glorious indoor "garden" conjured from luminous eighteenth-century Chinese wallpaper painted green. She designed the steel-and-brass bed and tented it with an extravagant taffeta baldachin. A green-and-white taffeta stripe covers Louis XVI chairs. A dressing mirror of Tula metalwork rests on the floor.

~ above ~

In her bedroom at Château de Mouton, Baroness de Rothschild displays a collection of English and Dutch brushes from the seventeenth-century against an eighteenth-century Chinese paper panel.

~ right ~

An illustration in a sixteenth-century Italian book inspired the stunning red-and-blue tile floor design in the vast living room at Château de Mouton. An elegant assortment of seventeenth- and eighteenth-century chairs stand like sentinels guarding an important collection of twentieth-century paintings and sculptures.

ANNETTE & SAMUEL REED

1966

This charming, traditional family grouping—of Samuel Pryor Reed, Annette Reed, their daughter Beatrice, and their Lhasa Apso, Toby, assembled in a beautiful living room adorned with eighteenth-century treasures—seems out of time with the social revolution of the mid-1960s swirling just outside. The young woman in the Rotari portrait hanging on pale green walls looks surprisingly contemporary with the other posers. The Dutch painted-leather screen, silk brocade sofa, Aubusson rug, and generous silver tankard overflowing with flowers help set the pervasive mood of calm formality.

~ above right ~

A beguiling trompe l'oeil of books and objects painted by Mrs. Reed is unmasked by a map hung in front of it. A crisply engineered art portfolio becomes a foil for the comfortable antique armchairs, marquetry box, and leopard rug. A mirrored bar is sequestered in the closet.

~ below right ~

An austere painting of the facade of a building and stark black obelisks contrast strikingly with the exuberant plaster work on the fireplace. Leather-bound books in the shelves and atop a table give a richness and luster that is echoed by the leather-covered eighteenth-century armchair in front of the fireplace.

LORD & LADY ELIOT

1966

Even if Ismail Merchant and James Ivory, in their ultimate genius, were doing the casting, who could imagine a more winning combination of players and place than Lord and Lady Eliot at home in their romantic family mansion, Port Eliot. The ninth Earl of Saint Germans, Lord Eliot's father, gave his son the seven-thousand-acre estate in Cornwall when he was twenty. Steeped in four hundred years of ancestral tradition, the battlemented house is chockablock with distinguished portraits of Eliots, many by Sir Joshua Reynolds. The Eliots await their guests in a splendid formal dining room on one of their frequent house party weekends. The table is set with a gleaming array of elaborate old family silver, part of a large collection. Many of the presentation pieces were given as wedding gifts by estate tenants. The Irish linen tablecloth was acquired in the 1850s by an Eliot who was Lord Lieutenant of Ireland.

~ above ~

An eruption of flame-colored poppies and blue lupines enlivens the dimly lit hall lined with stern black busts of notable eighteenth-century statesmen, including William Pitt the Younger. An early landscape view of Plymouth, England, by Sir Joshua Reynolds hangs on glowing crimson damask walls.

~ above ~

The fine family portrait in the Eliots' extensive collection by Sir Joshua Reynolds—Lady Jemima Cornwallis, with her son Lord Broome—hangs in a small, pale, very pretty drawing room. A collection of Minton plates echoes the delicate green and cream in the ravishing painting, as do a silk damask sofa and pillows.

DORIS DUKE

1966

Doris Duke, the American tobacco heiress, has satisfied two of her passions in "Shangri-La," the fantastical Persian palace she created in Hawaii. The first is the ocean, which sweeps in and out just in front, and the second is Muslim art. Here, she displays an astounding collection of aesthetic riches. Persian, Indian, Moroccan, Egyptian, Syrian, and Turkish motifs blend seamlessly among her treasures. The atmosphere is remarkably exotic—being there is like taking a magic carpet to *A Thousand and One Nights*. There are recreations in miniature of the Mogul gardens of Lahore, and twin staircases of five waterfalls apiece which descend to a luxurious Persian swimming pool pavilion. Here, wide beds swing on bronze chains embellished with Indian baubles. Overhead, a stenciled ceiling adds another layer of richness. Blue-and-white faience outlines the entrance. A colonnade of slender, elegantly worked pillars delimiting the porch reflects in the adjoining pool.

In a dining room fit for a sultan's palace, a magnificent crystal chandelier with electric candles casts hundreds of reflections on a low Indian bed that serves as a dining table. Guests repose on velvet hassocks. A procession of splendid faience panels embellishes striped Indian-cotton-covered walls. Illuminated alcoves display Persian plates, ewers, and flagons to the right of an ecclesiastical chimneypiece. In the foreground sparkle prisms from a tall nineteenth-century crystal candelabrum made by Baccarat for Persian aristocrats.

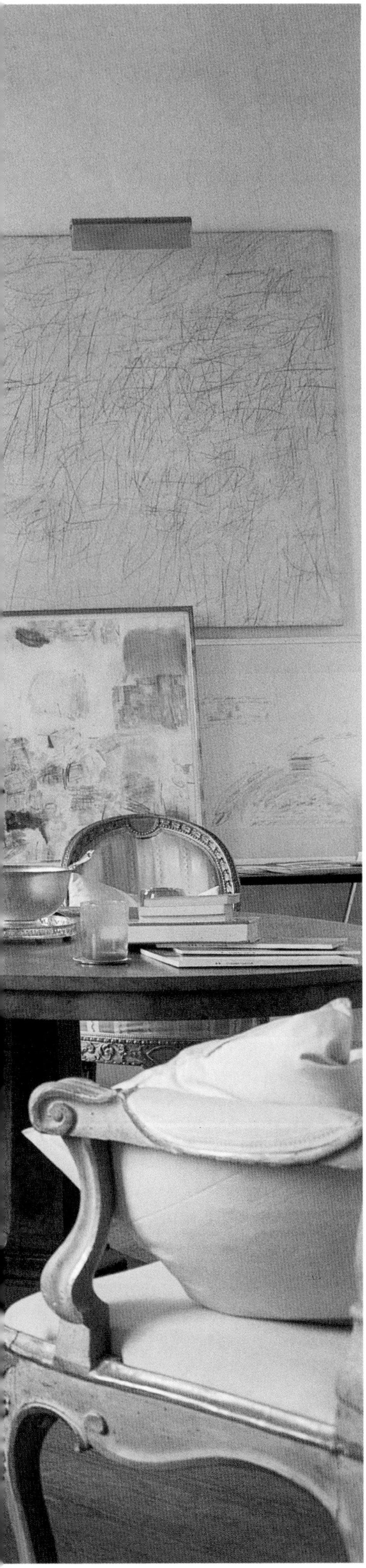

TATIANA & CY TWOMBLY

1966

The American abstract painter Cy Twombly got his first taste of Rome in the mid-1950s—and he never looked back. Two strokes of good fortune befell him. First, he allied himself with the illustrious patron and modern art collector Barone Giorgio Franchetti, who owned part interest in a gallery where Mr. Twombly became a regular exhibitor. Second, he met the baron's sister, Tatiana, and in 1958 married her. They live in an apartment in a Roman palazzo built for a seventeenth-century member of the Borgia family. The voluminous rooms, long enfilades, and grand proportions suit Mr. Twombly's enormous paintings. He stripped away centuries of paint to unveil a shell of white-washed walls and pale blue doors with silver moldings. A passionate interest in Greek and Roman history and mythology is reflected in his array of classical busts and statues, which act as stylistic and chromatic foils to his art. The Twomblys relax in their living room filled with antique Italian painted chairs, busts, and a painting by Robert Rauschenberg propped against one by Mr. Twombly.

~ above ~

A Roman bust is dwarfed by one of Cy Twombly's large paintings, casually propped against a refined antique Italian bench with a gilded and painted frame of exquisite grace.

~ left ~

An astonishing Italian Empire bed, featuring a headboard of asymmetrical columns topped with golden chalices, is swathed in Mongolian fox. Two equally palatial gilded, claw-footed Italian Empire chairs face each other across a round table. On the wall hangs a Cy Twombly painting inspired by Raphael's *School of Athens*.

DONNA MARELLA AGNELLI

1967

Once a proud rococo hunting lodge, Villa Agnelli, built in 1699 in the foothills of the Italian Alps and owned by the Agnelli family for more than a century, suffered bomb damage during World War II. Its salvation came in the person of Donna Marella Agnelli, a Neopolitan princess with an American mother; Donna Marella enthusiastically championed its restoration and renovation after her marriage to Giovanni Agnelli, chairman of Fiat. Beguiled by its mountain setting and fanciful design by Filippo Juvara, who was architect at the Court of Turin, she enlisted craftsmen from the nearby town of Villar Perosa in Piedmont to collaborate with a team of international experts. They restored the painted wall decorations in the *salone dipinto* (painted room), where Donna Marella is seated, and throughout the house. She also lavished care and attention on the gardens, a blaze of pink and red roses, which are at their height during September, the month the Agnellis and their children are in residence.

~ above ~

Painted chinoiserie panels emblazon the walls between the arched windows and doors in this magnificent gilt-scrolled gallery. The gallery benefits from double illumination: sunlight floods in from the tall windows, and candlelight glows from a line of chandeliers. Eighteenth-century silver consoles and painted antique chairs punctuate the space.

ANTENOR PATIÑO

1968

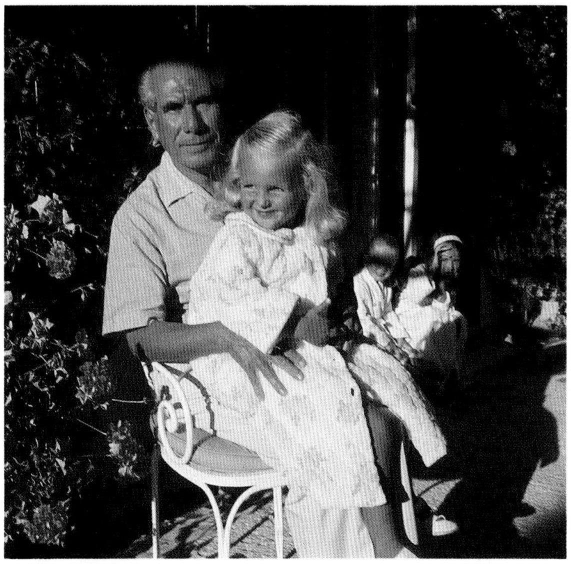

Antenor Patiño, shown with his granddaughter Cristina Schneider, lavished part of the riches from his Bolivian tin mines on his summer country house in Portugal—an extravagant testament to the fine eye and connoisseurship of its owner. Paintings by Goya, El Greco, and Cranach seem no more remarkable in this dazzling setting than the priceless seventeenth- and eighteenth-century French furniture and objets d'art that abound. A graceful and ornate library, the triumph of the house, is lined with leather-bound, gold-tooled books from the royal collections of France and Spain. A richly encrusted eighteenth-century French writing table on a Savonnerie carpet keeps pace with the gold chinoiserie decorations on the columns and the gilt-edge paneled ceiling.

~ above ~

This charmingly painted anteroom is surely one of the most magnificent cinemas in all of Europe. Energetic equestrian portraits of eighteenth-century rulers gallop around the walls.

~ above ~

Blue-and-white tiles in a majestic trompe l'oeil of architectural elements vividly set off a superb collection of etchings, *Los Caprichos,* by Goya. Drawings of the family add a charming and welcome note of informality.

~ above ~

The grandeur of the salon is redoubled by its reflection in a splendidly ornate mirror over the mantel. A magnificent clock displayed on the mantel boasts, surprisingly, an ormolu rhinoceros. A remarkable Beauvais tapestry depicting the adventures of Don Quixote appears to go on forever, as do the patterned gold ceiling and swirling gilt sconces. The rich colors of the upholstery echo those in the tapestry.

~ left ~

Three sea gods rendered in blue-and-white tile overlook a pearly, shell-shaped fountain and the azure water of the pool. The refreshing cool of the long, pink arcade, with its terra-cotta tile floor, provides a pleasant setting for outdoor lunches served on a Florentine table with a *pietra dura* top.

MICA ERTEGÜN

1969

Mica Ertegün, copartner in the decorating firm Mac II, teamed up with architect Joseph G. Merz to satisfy her fantasy of a Manhattan town house that was more about space and light than tradition and decor. Tension between a conventional stair rail ascending to the second floor and the carefully choreographed curve of a concrete divider wall enlivens the free-flowing living area. She specified yards and yards of white walls in anticipation of the fun she would have filling them with her prized collection of modern art, including works by Ellsworth Kelly, Magritte, and Jack Youngerman. On frequent travels with her husband, Ahmet Ertegün, president of Atlantic Records, Mica searches for objects of artistry and whimsy to embellish her ascetic interior.

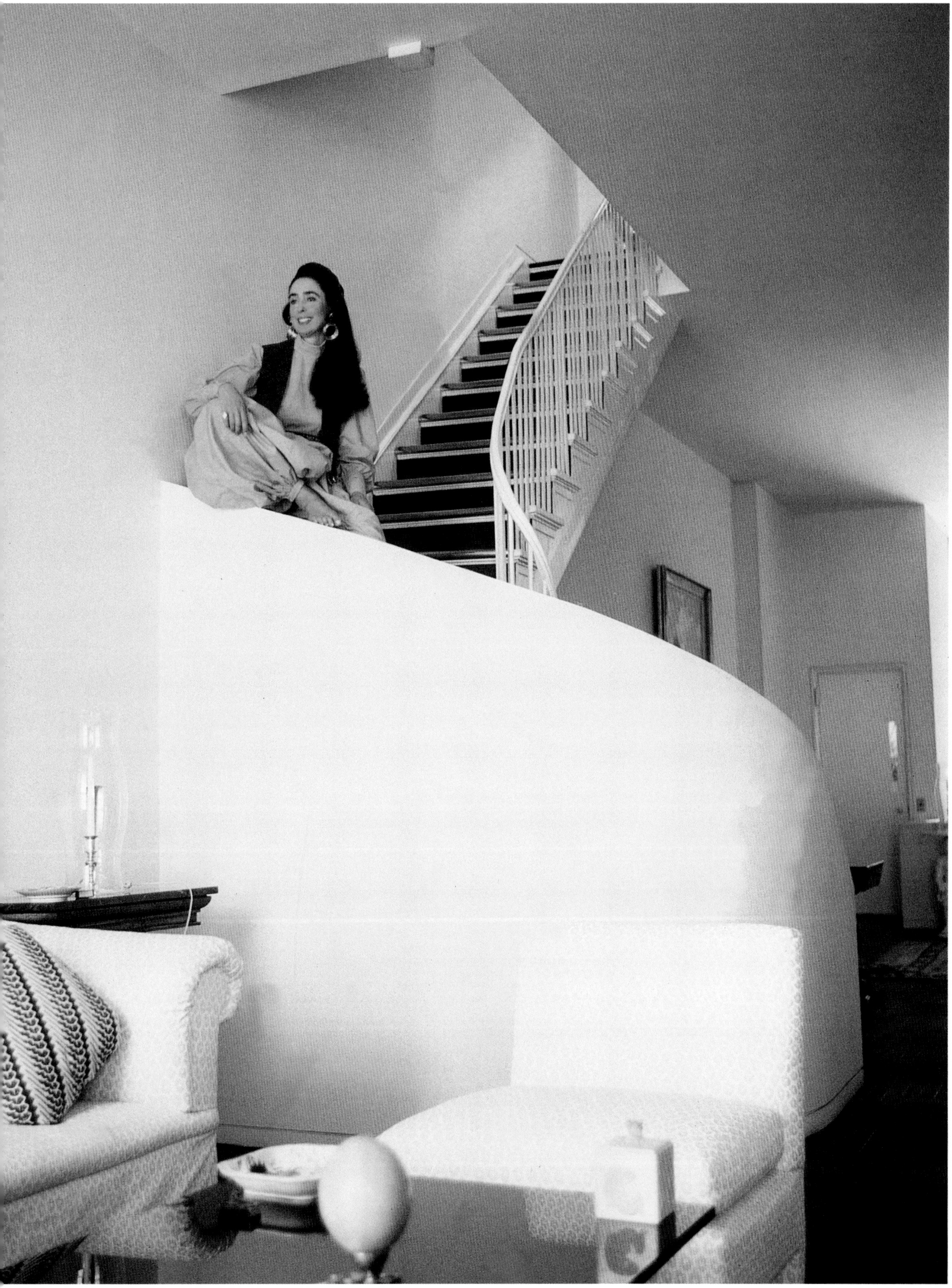

JANE HOLZER

1969

"Baby Jane" Holzer and her living room epitomize the fun, the energy, the outrageousness, and the freedom of mod living. A renowned pop art collection mixes ebulliently with sprightly, anything-but-dowdy eighteenth-century pieces. Lacking only the rose between her teeth, Mrs. Holzer, in her Sant'Angelo gypsy dress and piquant barefoot pose, somehow brings all the lively and disparate elements of the room together. An abstract painting by Larry Zox and an equally colorful thirteen-foot-high screen covered in eighteenth-century Chinese wallpaper seem locked in a tug-of-war for the space. Two stools covered in a lacy white fabric were originally ordered from India by Queen Victoria. In the foreground a table of polished petrified wood holds a collection of seashells.

GLORIA VANDERBILT

1970

A high-voltage passion for creating collages inspired Gloria Vanderbilt to transform her bedroom into a rich, exotic fantasy world of color and texture. Ironically, the end result is anything but naive or old-fashioned, as one might expect from such a lathering of American quilts. Rather, it is redolent of mystery and sophistication, with riffs of seraglios and sultans. Each surface is a work of art in itself. The walls and ceiling Miss Vanderbilt covered with two dozen handmade American patchwork quilts from her extensive collection. She executed the patchwork floor by painstakingly fitting fabric scraps with no overlap and varnishing them to a high gloss. The silk draperies she left unlined so the sunlight would filter through, giving the illusion of stained glass.

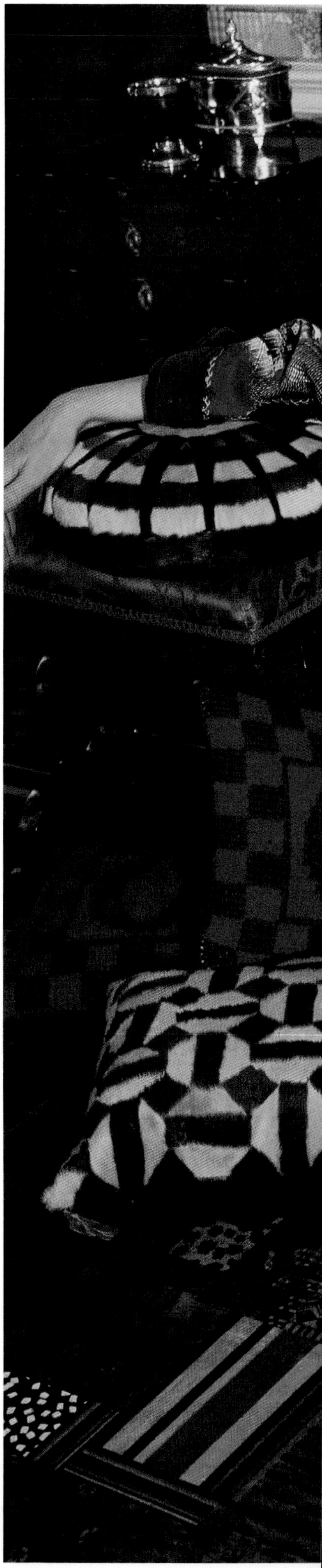

With the exception of white enamel moldings, patchwork covers every inch of the walls, floor, and ceiling of this remarkable bedroom. The framed collages *Christmas Present* and *Cavalier* by Miss Vanderbilt, which hang over the bed, are fashioned of fabric, aluminum foil, and cutout colored paper. A rare Elizabethan jewelry chest, a red lacquer chinoiserie table, and a seventeenth-century French petit-point bench seem perfectly at home with all the bits and pieces of Americana.

BETTY & FRANÇOIS CATROUX

1970

Who would guess that this dashing op art apartment resides inside a seventeenth-century *hôtel particulier* in Paris? Designated a historical monument, the building isn't allowed to be altered structurally. Despite this constraint, interior designer François Catroux, pictured with his wife, Betty, wanted to make his own design statement—and that most certainly did not include elegant moldings and exquisite plaster work. He hid the unwelcome architectural detailing behind temporary walls and ceilings. In the master bedroom he created a spectacular op art bed with a boldly magnified yellow-and-white stripe that flows without interruption from canopy to spread to rug. From left to right are sculptural abstractions by Munari, Tomasello, and Duarte.

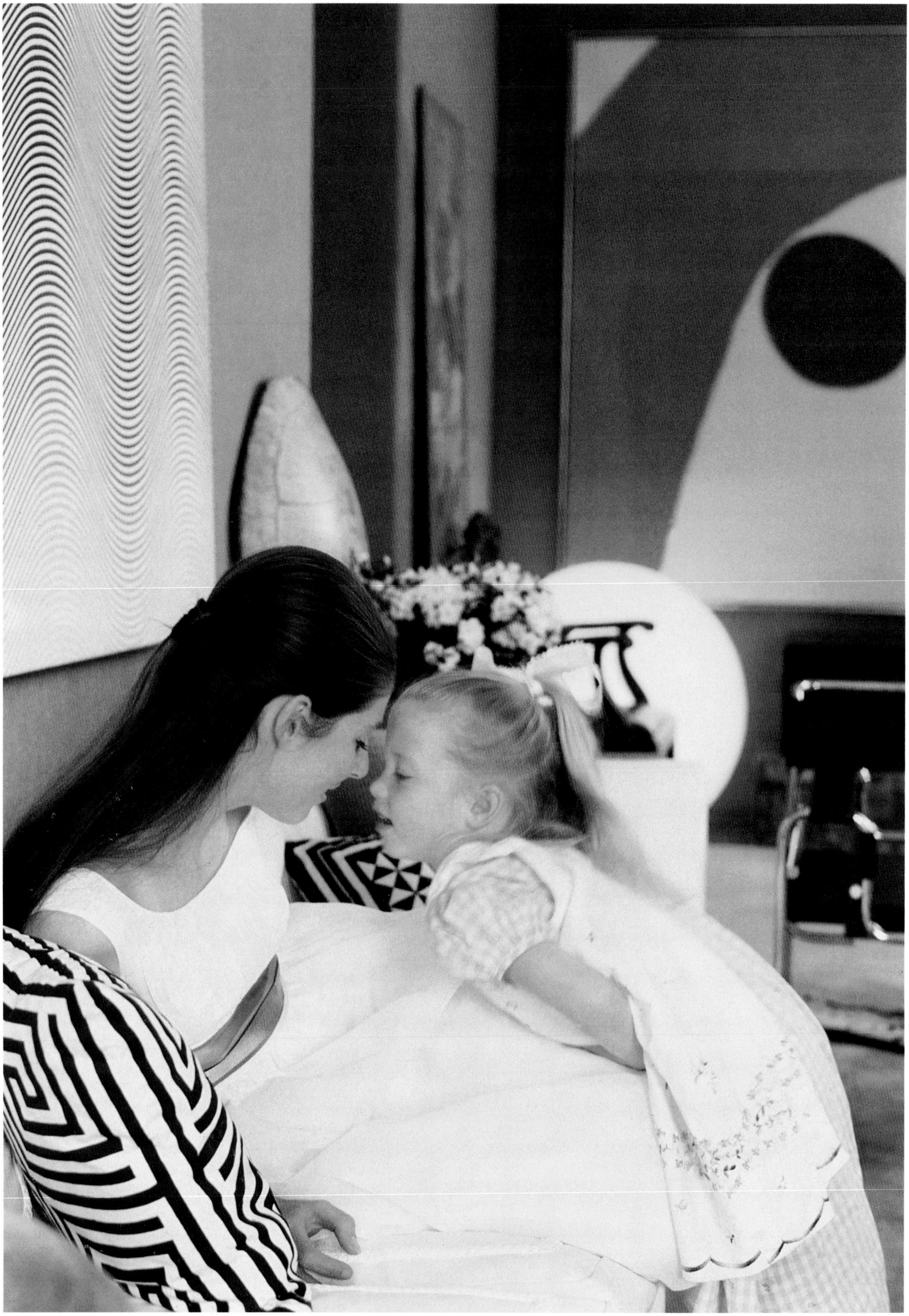

GWENDOLYN WARNER

1970

Gwendolyn Warner successfully commingles color, pattern, and texture without sending a busy signal. The carefully controlled proportions and subdued tobacco wall color keep everything looking serenely cool. Pictured forehead to forehead with her daughter Laura, Mrs. Warner displays a flair for juxtapositions by playing the sharp black-and-white Indian motifs on the pillows off against the vibrating stripes of a Bridget Riley painting hanging on the wall behind them. An overscaled globe of a lamp and a large albino tortoise shell are used as counterpoints to the bold circles in *Juice,* a painting by Jules Olitski. The remarkable, predominantly American painting collection on display in Mrs. Warner's understated California house (which was designed by her husband, architect Jack Lionel Warner) comes from her father, Robert A. Rowan.

~ above ~

A blue-and-white theme is rendered in a fresh California way, with a white pique bedspread and a canvas baldachin lined with a flower print echoed on the cushions and armchair. The rug was custom made in Portugal for the bedroom.

~ left ~

A dramatic juxtaposition of cultures and forms—a Ptolemaic head from a sarcophagus superimposed on a Navajo rug—keys the color scheme of this restfully monochromatic room. Chinese silk panels flank an eighteenth-century French marble mantelpiece, and a low Coromandel screen stands in front of it.

LYNN & STEVEN JACOBSON

1970

For Lynn and Steven Jacobson, the next best thing to taking up residence in a fashionable art gallery was transforming their apartment into one. The Jacobsons thrive on living on the hard edge. They commissioned their friend Richard Ohrbach not only to decorate their digs but also to create big, bold pieces of graphic art for it. Color and pattern vibrate against a calm sea of subdued dark blue on the walls. A supersize, transparent assemblage of squares and stripes by Ohrbach skips across the windows. A rainbow-striped fabric gives zest to a staid Louis XV armchair. Reflections of the hot colors bounce off a steel-and-glass fireplace, a collection of Edwardian and Victorian silver, and a classic Italian Arco lamp. A frenetic blue-and-white op art rug enlivens the floor.

~ above ~

This breakfast room would get anyone going in the morning. Diagonal stripes of hot color slash across white walls. A ribbon of color somersaults across a painting by Peter Mitchel. In the window a mobile of glass, plastic, mirror, and steel by Richard Ohrbach twirls slowly. The familiar lines of classic Saarinen chairs help to lower the temperature.

~ right ~

"In-the-pink" walls, floor, and ceiling jump-start an optimistic mood in this zinger of a bathing temple. The dressing room, in the foreground, is given sparkle by tiny lights encased in the Lucite pedestal legs of the vanity. In the bathroom beyond, an assemblage of colored plastic panels covers the window.

EVANGELINE BRUCE

1970

Living abroad for eighteen years—in Germany, France, and England—as the wife of a United States ambassador offered Evangeline Bruce many advantages. Not least among them was the chance to ferret out furniture and art that would, with the return of the natives, gloriously decorate the Washington, D.C., house that is now their home. Mrs. David K. E. Bruce has kept her large living room cozy and personal by dividing the space into a series of small sitting areas. Here, art and objects collected in Europe mix with subtly colored fabrics and rugs. Mrs. Bruce sits in front of a charming seventeenth-century Dutch panel, one of four she found in Paris. She discovered the wonderfully ornate white-and-gold English Regency chairs with their resplendent gold silk upholstery in a country antique shop in England.

~ above ~

A large Bessarabian rug with a winsomely pastoral motif makes a surprising and successful foil for quietly traditional furniture and accessories in the living room. Overhung with a Flemish painting, the elaborate and stunning mantel was a find from a house in Charleston, South Carolina.

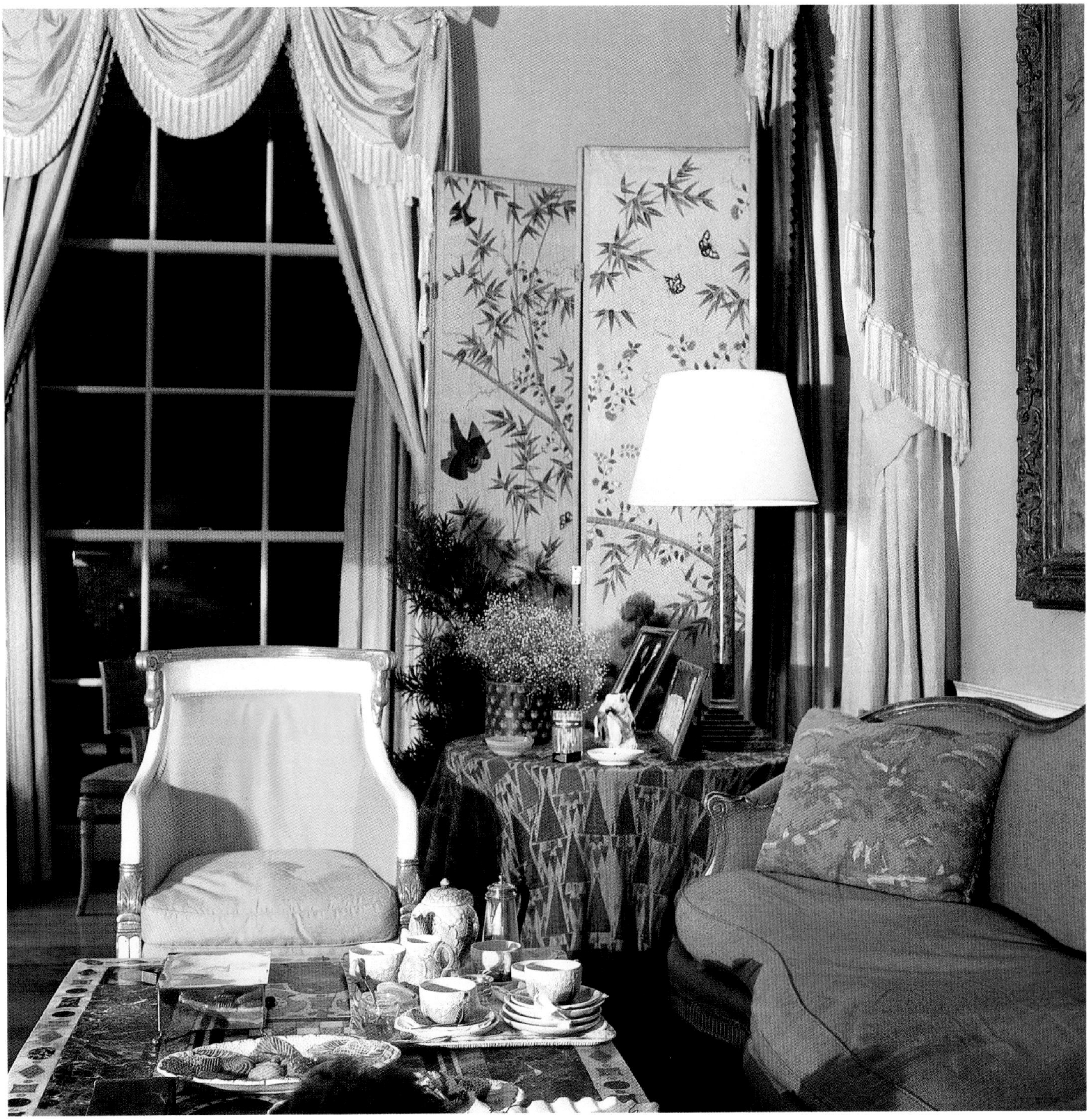

~ above ~

The Bruce's large living room is artfully arranged with cozy corners. A fearless use of color—lime-tasseled draperies, watermelon-hued walls, and a gold chair—takes the edge off the formality. A patterned eighteenth-century Middle Eastern table skirt contrasts smartly with a lyrical Chinese paper screen.

GLORIA STEINEM

1970

For a free-lance writer, a study of one's own is the most important room of all. Here, she spends the most hours and expends the most energy. In her brownstone floor-through Gloria Steinem allocated for her professional self a room that quadruples as an office, a library, a conference room, and a sanctuary for tête-à-têtes. She

carved up the rest of the high-ceilinged space with a sleeping balcony that spans a curl-up nest of an alcove swathed in Indian scarves—well-loved reminders of a two-year sojourn in India. The balcony was made from balusters and columns belonging to an old front porch found at a wrecking company. Big pillows brightened with Indian prints extend the seating circle onto the floor. The apartment's verve, color, and energy perfectly mirror its owner.

VIVA CHAVEZ
VIVA LA CAUSA
Kennedy
LOUVRE

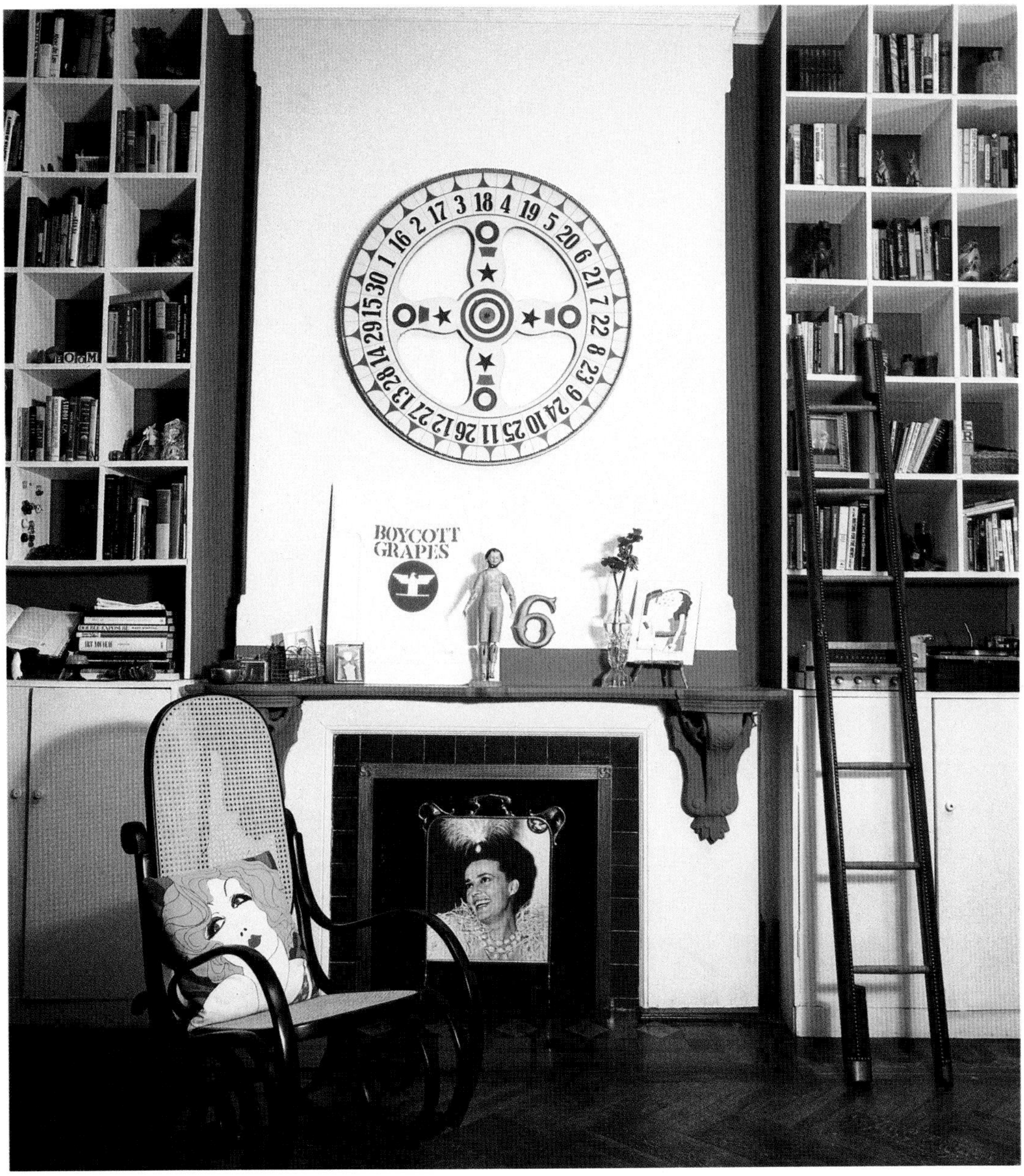

~ above ~

Serving as repositories for objects and books, neat, white, twelve-inch cubicles climb bright blue walls on either side of the fireplace. A portable library ladder makes their height functional. A photograph of the actress Jeanne Moreau dominates the fireplace; above it is a country roulette wheel.

~ left ~

A blue-and-white cotton flame stitch leaps from wicker Bermuda bed to walls to draperies. Blue-on-red printed curtains at the windows add visual contrast and depth. A large white cupboard doubles as a bulletin board for posters, photographs, signs, and buttons. A white flokati rug and a Thonet rocker pull the room together.

DOROTHEA ELMAN

1970

"A moonscape" is how architect Paul Rudolph describes the surreal apartment he created for Dorothea and Lee Elman. In the living room, he threw away all traditional ideas of furnishing, lighting, and accessorizing—and substituted his own radical concepts. A seating assemblage of pillows of different shapes and heights grows organically out of the shaggy white rug. Lucite table tops and bases seem to disappear into thin air, leaving coaster-like mirrors floating like extraterrestrials. Silvered bare bulbs hang from the ceiling in classical regularity, while uplights recessed in the seating cast a moody glow. Color has been concentrated in the hall in a series of four vivid Plexiglas panels that Mr. Rudolph terms "light paintings." Mrs. Elman lounges with her daughter Alexandra in this unique and truly modern space.

Mirrors and more mirrors turn this dining room into a hall of glitter. Mylar-covered chairs and a spiderweb canopy of tiny lights add to the glamour, as does a row of stout candles marching up the center of the glimmering table top.

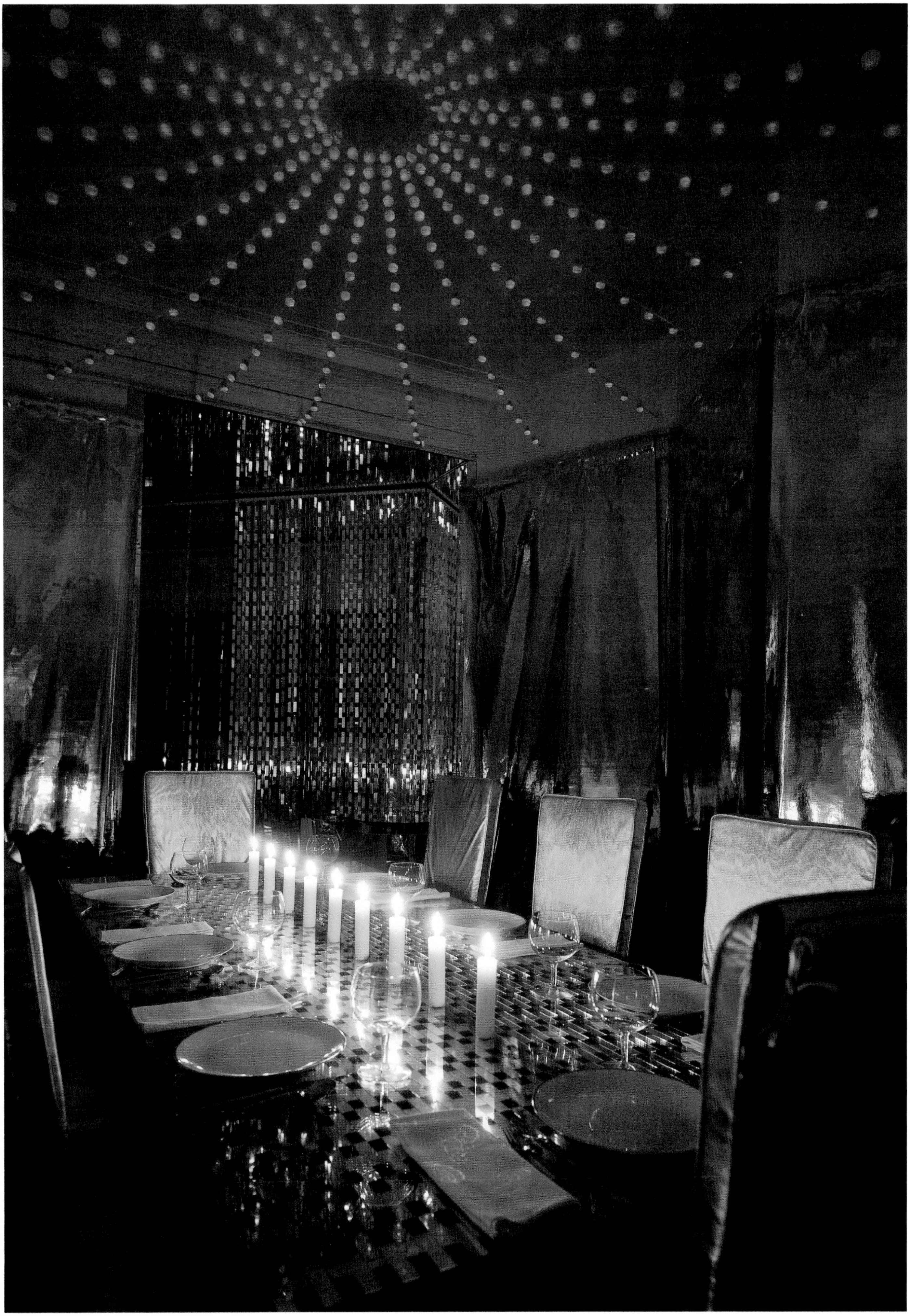

CONTESSA SUSANNA RATTAZZI

1971

Contessa Susanna Rattazzi, a writer who usually resides in her native Italy, wanted a New York apartment that was very American. Her daring solution was to persuade Mark Hampton, Robert Denning, and Vincent Fourcade, leading decorators all, to work on her project as a team. Though each has his own distinctive style, what

Messrs. Hampton, Denning, and Fourcade share is a love of pattern and opulence. Contessa Rattazzi contributed her own love of comfort to the mix. She wanted friends to drop by unannounced—an anomaly in New York—and to feel welcome and at home. In the easygoing living room a white arched doorway and white ceiling provide a crisp architectural edge to the flamboyance of pattern on pattern. The dual palette—blue and white, peach and yellow—echoes the beautiful Turner over the sofa. The walls, upholstered in a padded blue basket-print cotton, are set off by a rare, antique Persian rug with a blue ground.

~ above ~

At night the dining room becomes the poker room, and the round table, simply set here for a quiet luncheon, turns into the playing table. A softly curved fringed valance echoes the arch framing one of a set of old paintings of the four seasons.

~ above ~

Beyond the canopy the next level in bed decoration is a fabric-covered dome. This inventive treatment offers the added practical advantage of making a small room seem larger. A splendid nineteenth-century mahogany-and-gilt bed was placed at an angle to further heighten its already high drama.

ELIZABETH VAGLIANO

1971

Alexander Vagliano, a banker, was a closet modernist living in Connecticut. When he moved to a traditional prewar apartment in New York City with his wife and three children, he let his imagination run loose. He tore down walls and created flexible spaces delimited with pivoting floor-to-ceiling walnut panels. He made a game of three-dimensional geometry, having fun with a battery of modern materials, including plastic, stainless steel, and neon. Elizabeth Vagliano relaxes in a custom-made seating area made of exotic wooden blocks. Pots of hot pink tulips recessed into table cubes add a tonic of color to the monochromatic scheme, as does a chartreuse fiberglass sculpture by Gio Pomodoro. Modern art is a major player in this spare, no-nonsense living area, lighted as if it were a gallery.

~ above ~

A unique suspension bed hangs by stainless steel cables from a frame attached to the ceiling. A subtle marbled monochromatic painting hangs on one wall; the richly grained wood-paneled closets cover the other. A shaggy white carpet gives needed warmth and texture to the otherwise ascetic bedroom.

~ right ~

There is nothing square about this space-age dining room. A ringtoss of a neon lighting fixture hovers over a round plastic table and a circular steel floor. A pass-through into the kitchen seems to float on the pebble-embedded wall like an eclipsed moon.

LEE RADZIWILL

1971

Leave it to an American to figure out how to combat the dreary, gray English climate: with a battalion of flowers—fresh, woven, painted, and printed. Lee Radziwill, here accompanied by her Pekingese and golden Labrador retriever, turned Turville Grange, an eighteenth-century country house forty-five miles from London, into a joyous paradise of color, pattern, and texture. In the dining room Sicilian scarves, which have been lacquered, metamorphose into inventive and lively wall coverings; flower-wreathed painted panels by Lila de Nobili are superimposed on them.

~ above ~

This airy, contemporary pool house, designed to suggest an overturned ship with its keel pointing to the sky, is in striking contrast to the eighteenth-century flavor of the main house. A clerestory and a battery of French doors overlooking an apple orchard bring in abundant natural light. Blond ash furniture and white upholstery stand out crisply against the herringbone brick floors.

~ above right ~

It's difficult to imagine not feeling happy in this exuberant garden room. Beautiful exotic birds in romantic old-fashioned cages savor a vista of glorious flowers rampant on matching wall and upholstery fabric and abloom in jardinieres and pots.

~ below right ~

What more delicious luxury than enough space and the bonus of a fireplace to transform the front hall into a warm, cozy sitting room? Flowers are everywhere: in old botanicals mounted on walls covered with silk shantung, on the chair upholstery and the rug, and arranged in expansive bouquets on the tables.

JAN COWLES

1971

Modern architecture rarely stars in a prewar Fifth Avenue apartment, but when a talent of Paul Rudolph's stature creates it, signs of his facility with space can be seen everywhere. Rudolph's clients, Gardner Cowles, the founder of *Look* magazine, and his wife, Jan, gave the modernist master a free hand. In the library Rudolph eliminated conventional doors and walls, and embraced the space with a curved aubergine wall of bookcases. The vistas Rudolph opened up give full play to the Cowles's spectacular collection of modern art, including a Roy Lichtenstein painting in the hall. Selected by French decorator François Catroux, the furniture includes rose leather captain's chairs and a French game table. The large aubergine rug was made of squares of cowhide. Jan Cowles indulges in a favorite avocation: arranging flowers.

Show-stopping glamour is the theme of this bathroom, which could double as a Hollywood star's dressing room. Small, round mirrors on a white ground create a wall of shimmer and sparkle, on which *Red Bathrobe,* a Jim Dine lithograph, hangs. The mirror theme repeats—this time on string—in a window curtain and a divider wall. A shaggy white rug and a curvaceous upholstered chair serve as welcome antidotes to all the hard surfaces.

DEEDA BLAIR

1972

Old-fashioned comfort and new-fashioned airiness meet in Deeda Blair's Georgian-style brick town house in Georgetown. The wife of William McCormick Blair, Jr., a former ambassador and a director of the Kennedy Center for the Performing Arts, she didn't want to hand over the refurbishing of her house to a professional only to become a sideline cheerleader, so she persuaded decorator Billy Baldwin to join her as mentor and collaborator. She masterminded their joint effort from her workroom, where flowers vie with watercolors and porcelain for space on a green-painted French desk. She chose many Baldwin hallmarks—skirted tables, Coromandel screens, off-white walls and floors—but shunned others, such as his signature chintzes. It's hard to imagine any guest not feeling at home in these rooms, which are refreshingly easy with an infectious, buoyant charm.

The large and spectacular Coromandel screen that enriches one wall of the living room is the triumph of a fine eye. Mrs. Blair found it in pieces in Paris and had it reconstructed. A skirted table, prettily covered eighteenth-century chairs, and a white sofa create an appealingly understated look.

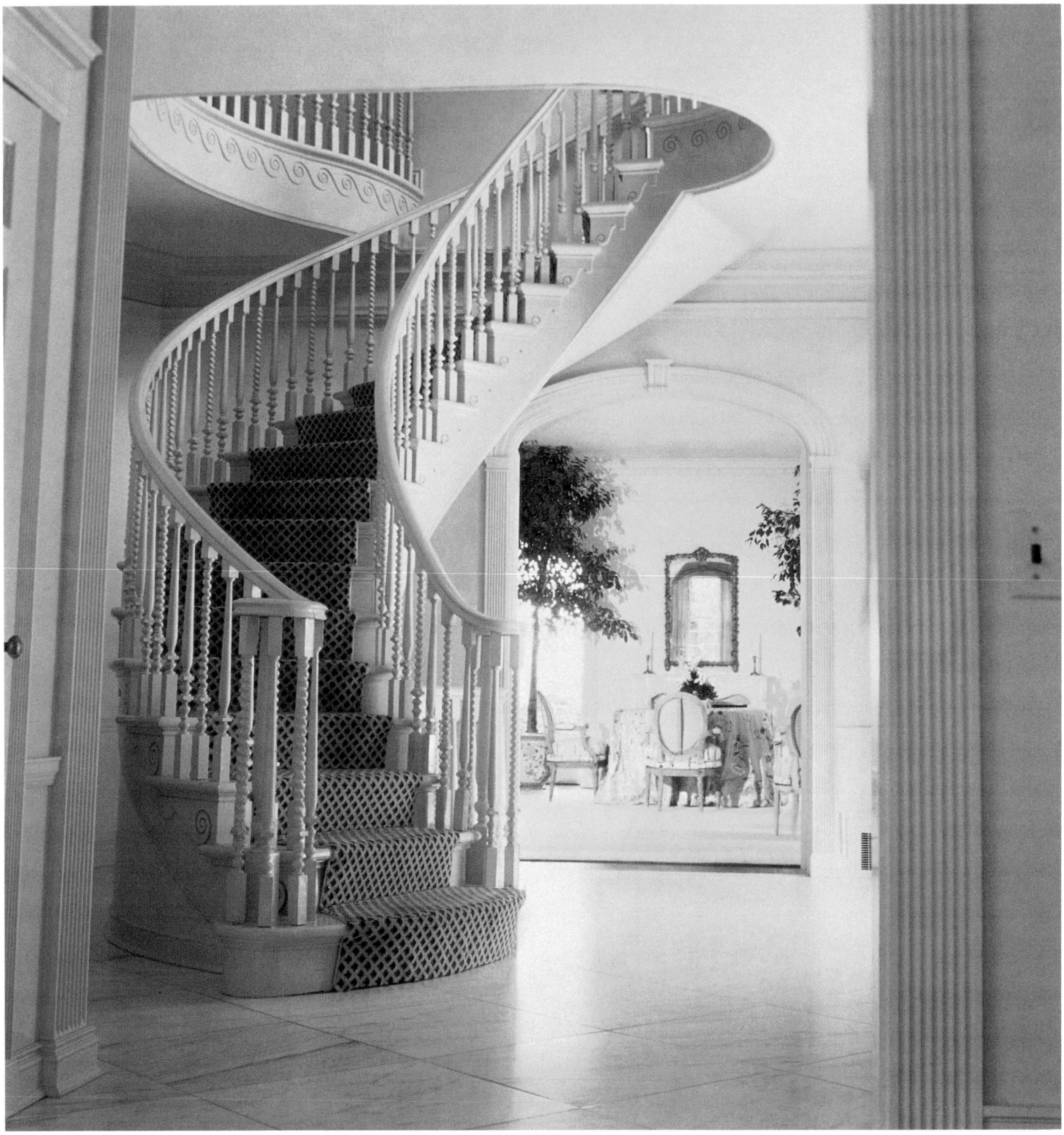

~ above ~

The sweeping center staircase performs with all the drama of an oversize sculpture. Double doors with handsome classical architectural detailing lead from the white marble entrance hall into a charming dining room, where oversize trees bring the outside greenery in.

~ above ~

The curtain treatment on this graceful eighteenth-century bed, with its ascending rows of jaunty green-and-white tassels, is a delight. Off-white textured silk draperies were hand painted in Hong Kong with a jocund floral design by Mrs. Blair. The sheen of the sherbet green table skirt competes with the high gloss on the white lacquer floor.

GLORIA GUINNESS

1972

Mexican-born Gloria Guinness wanted her house above the Bay of Acapulco to be a showcase for the art and handicrafts of her country, as well as a popular way station for children, grandchildren, and friends from America and Europe. The openness of the space and the ease of the furnishings literally invite the surplus of guests this legendary hostess revels in. In the round room—named "the palapa," a word she coined, for its domed ceiling of palm fronds—islands of concrete banquettes, softened with handwoven cushions, and generously sized wicker armchairs are dotted about a sea of rough concrete painted and lacquered to a high sheen. All the furniture and accessories in this airy room—which is like a great hall and opens to the terrace and the views—were handmade in Mexico.

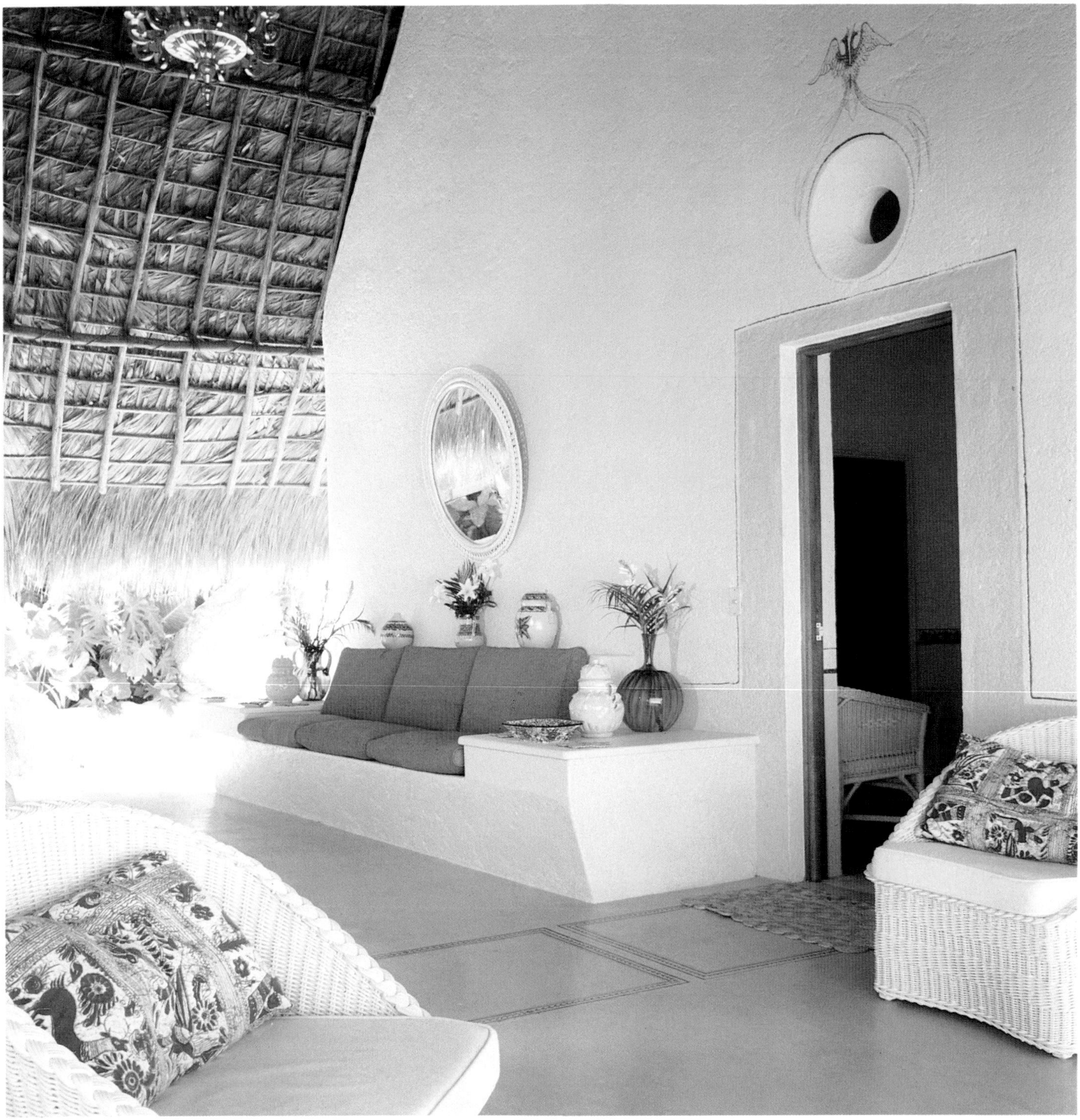

~ above ~

Separate guest cottages with whitewashed walls smoothed by hand allow visitors to be totally independent. Separating two bedrooms and baths, the thatch-roofed terraces double as living rooms and breakfast areas, with built-in sofas and tables of painted concrete, refrigerators, and bars.

~ right ~

The only antique in the house—a Colonial statue of a saint with porcelain eyes—resides in a niche in the dining room. Mrs. Guinness's collection of Mexican pottery energizes the room. A locally woven textile on the table echoes the blue-and-white theme; a straw rug is made of *petates*, handwoven peasant sleep mats. Simple hand-carved dining chairs are finds from a nearby market.

NONIE & THOMAS SCHIPPERS

1972

Cincinnati is home to the traveling road show of Nonie and Thomas Schippers. As music director of the Cincinnati Symphony Orchestra, the peripatetic Mr. Schippers alights in Ohio for regular stints, but frequently goes abroad with his wife to fulfill his other obligations as music director of the Spoleto Festival in central Italy and director of special projects for Italian radio and television in Milan. With such a kinetic life, tranquillity and comfort topped the Schipperses' list of requirements for the interior of a rambling Victorian house. With the help of decorator Paul Dorsett, Mrs. Schippers gracefully integrated a fine collection of Chinese Chippendale furniture inherited from her mother, Mrs. Michael Grace Phipps. In the living room a spirited blue floral wallpaper works in concert with white textured sofas and chairs, white sailcloth curtains, and ubiquitous fresh flowers to achieve a relaxed, pretty space.

~ above ~

The many lives of the library include bridge (a favorite sport), and change-of-pace fireside dining. Faux leopard upholstery complements patterns in the rug and the fireplace tile. A treasured Lowestoft plate inspired the rich cobalt blue wall color.

~ left ~

White lattice-covered walls and ceiling turn the conservatory into a delightful, three-dimensional trellis. Not surprisingly, this room ranks as the favorite one in the house. White wicker chairs with green cushions take their color cue from an abundance of plants and flowers. The bonus of a fireplace makes this the preferred spot for after-concert suppers.

ENID HAUPT

1973

What better place for Enid Annenberg Haupt to be photographed than up a tree? A nature lover and a horticultural guru, she is also a connoisseur and a major art collector. The strong aesthetic side of her life is rivaled only by her celebrity—as a philanthropist (among many good deeds, she saved Wellington, a Virginia house once owned by George Washington, by donating a million dollars for its purchase). In her Palm Beach hideaway Mrs. Haupt exhibits her famed finesse at creating still lifes with art and orchids, her flowers of choice. The swirls and curls of a Louis XV console table make wonderful foils for a Mark Rothko painting; *Horse and Rider,* a bronze by Marino Marini; and a strikingly graphic pottery urn.

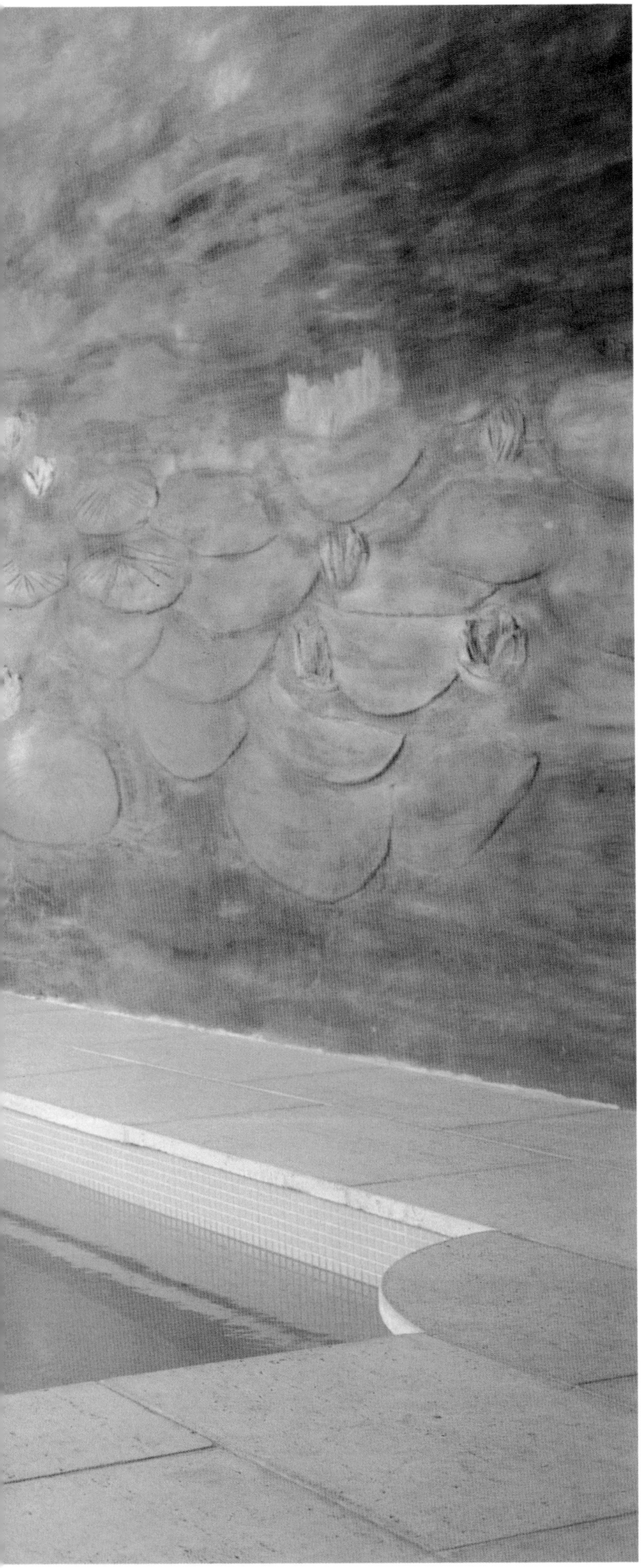

Claude Monet's *Nymphaes* series of water lily paintings is such a favorite of Mrs. Haupt's that she commissioned artist Charles Merrill to paint a fresco version on the wall beside the pool. An original hangs in her house. *Homo*, a powerful metal sculpture by Oskar Schlemmer, hangs in stark contrast on the adjacent wall.

JACQUELINE ONASSIS

1973

Like the universe in a grain of sand, an individual's interests and eye may be revealed in a still life of prized possessions. Jacqueline Onassis enjoys spending time in her comfortable library, surrounded by mementos of her life and travels. It is a favorite place to read, write letters, and visit informally with friends and family. The discrete background of the room is more about texture than pattern—red-and-white hand-blocked Indian cotton on the walls and straw matting on the floor. The comfortable brown velvet sofa is enlivened by

pillows made of Liberty silk scarves that Mrs. Onassis has collected over the years. The coffee table displays Mrs. Onassis's pleasures and treasures. A basket of fruit and another of tulips become vivid backdrops for worry beads from Greece; a delicately dried mushroom on a branch, carefully carried back from a trip to Angkor Wat; black coral found in the Yucatán peninsula; and Egyptian cats in bronze.

ANNE FORD UZIELLI

1973

The only thing that isn't jumping in this lively, modern apartment is its owner, Anne Ford Uzielli. A rip-roaring red lacquered wall ignites the lightning bolt freneticism of overscaled herringbone—red and white in the carpet, and black and white in the fur cushions on double-curved black-and-white lacquered stools. Energetic red-and-white pillows from Latin America fairly dance across the plain white sofas. To focus full attention on Robert Müller's Lucite-topped papier-mâché work over the fireplace, Mrs. Uzielli and decorator Charles Dear kept the understated mantel flush with the wall. Crisp geometric lamp bases reiterate the shiny Lucite theme.

KATHARINE GRAHAM

1973

Tradition with a twist distinguishes this comfortable, though formal, Georgetown house. Its owner is Katharine Graham, chairman of the board of the Washington Post Company, which publishes the *Washington Post* and *Newsweek,* and owns several radio and television stations—which helps explain the worldliness and sophistication of the decorative mix. Much of the fine English antique furniture she inherited from her father, Eugene Meyer, who purchased the *Post* in 1933. Mrs. Graham, who took over management of the *Post* from her late husband, Philip, in 1963, presided over its most celebrated epoch, the exposé of the Watergate break-in of June 1972. An art lover, she has wide-ranging interests in modern painting and a passion for Chinese furniture, rugs, and objects, passed on to her by her mother, a student of Chinese art.

~ above ~

The peaceful, plum-colored library, enlivened by a rug with a delightful image of Noah's Ark, makes an ideal retreat. Mrs. Graham's intriguingly disparate collection of art includes a striking Japanese Noh mask of carved and polychromed wood on the mantel, a painting by Diego Rivera above it, a vibrant Color Field painting by Morris Louis on the left-hand wall, and a magnificent Chinese horse on the coffee table.

~ above ~

The large living room fairly glows with its fiery red walls and draperies, and lustrous Chinese carpet. Panels from a Coromandel screen face each other above a stately trio of Philadelphia Chippendale chairs. An early-nineteenth-century gilt mirror overhangs an intricately sculpted marble mantel. On a table to the right sits Chinese tomb jade inherited from Mrs. Graham's mother.

FRANÇOISE & OSCAR DE LA RENTA

1969 ~ 1974

It's clear from their romantic, yet easy, Dominican vacation retreat and their comfortable, yet glamorous, New York duplex that Françoise and Oscar de la Renta know how to live well. In their house on the beach, unfettered by the urban grid, they indulge themselves in spaces that vault three stories without stopping. Their fabric choice is relaxed: natural canvas, handkerchief linen, batiks; in rugs they opt for barefoot-friendly sisal; in furniture they prefer free-and-easy bamboo. For their bedroom Mr. de la Renta designed a fantasy bed shaped like a Siamese temple. The New York apartment is all about superimposed pattern, pretty objects, fur (real and fake), sink-in sofas, cushions without end, rugs on carpeting, and a passion for blue and white.

~ above ~

The soaring spaces of a barnlike living room reveal the straightforward framing of the house. White canvas cushions cover bamboo furniture designed by Mr. de la Renta and made locally. Potted palms, ceiling fans, tortoise shells hanging above mahogany doors, and a veranda give an unmistakably tropical feel.

~ above ~

This bathroom is about relaxing, primping, and pampering, and enjoying palms, ferns, sunshine, and space. It is about big tubs and long soaks. It is a hedonist's dream, a flight from the dark, depressing confines of wintry urban living. It is not about compromise and making do.

~ above right ~

A blue-and-white wallscape makes a charming vista for diners. Two large porcelain plates hang above an assembly of porcelain: a jardiniere, a platter, lamps, carpet balls from an English game, candle holders, and garden stools. The wallpaper pretends to be blue-and-white tile. A crisp harlequin design on a needlepoint rug cools the pyrotechnics of pattern on pattern.

~ below right ~

A kaleidoscope of pattern in the monochromatic living room begins with an eighteenth-century tortoise shell box, inlaid with mother-of-pearl, on the desk, and ends with leopard velvet pillows on a fur-covered suede sofa. The painting is by Feito.

SPAIN—A HISTORY IN ART

MARCIA WEISMAN

1974

Every morning Mr. and Mrs. Frederick R. Weisman wake up to enjoy museum-class modern art in their contemporary glass-walled southern California house. Their extensive collection spills out into the garden, patios, and pool area. Marcia Weisman, seen in

the indoor patio behind a bronze by Jacques Lipchitz, carries her personal passion for art into her work. She teaches art classes, runs an art advisory service, and is the art consultant to the Mayo Clinic Foundation. The light, airy tree- and flower-filled indoor patio—a haven for unwinding and savoring art—opens onto the garden. Through the glass doors Mrs. Weisman's portrait by Andy Warhol is visible; on the round table is a wood sculpture by Max Ernst; hanging above, a mobile by Alexander Calder; and in the foreground, a wood-and-bronze sculpture by William Turnbull.

VALENTINO

1974

If you're Valentino, there's no such thing as too many beautiful objects, too much pattern, or too dramatic a decor. When the legendary Italian fashion designer became crowded out of his apartment by his exquisite—and growing—collections of furniture and accessories, he moved them—and himself—into a spacious villa near Rome on the Via Appia Antica. Here, he and Renzo Mongiardino, the esteemed Italian interior designer, combined their talents in the decoration. They created each room as a different stage set, but all share the overarching themes of glamour and exoticism. The team's wit and originality abound in tablescapes, still lifes, and fusillades of pattern on pattern. They are particularly fond of vignettes that evoke romantic places, such as Morocco, India, Turkey, and Egypt. Cleopatra would have felt right at home in this large and eclectic living room, with its fireplace housed in a porcelain pyramid, columns lining the walls, and a gold-trimmed day bed that could have been her barge.

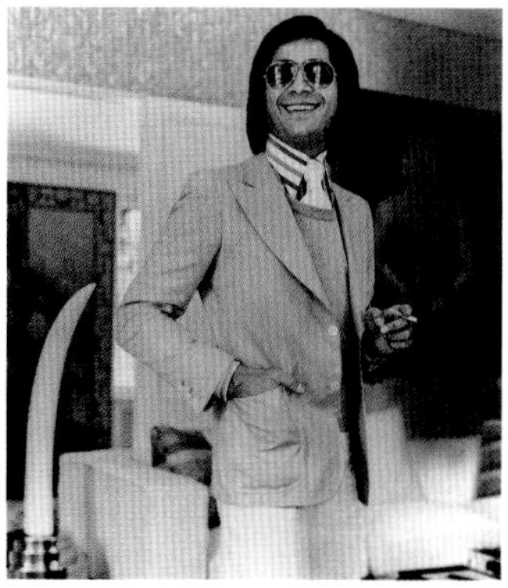

~ above ~

An illustration in an old Indian book inspired Valentino to design the fabric that covers the walls and ceiling of a small sitting room adjoining his bedroom and bath. Indian glass paintings make perfect foils for the busily patterned walls. A Moroccan carpet echoes the medallion motif of the fabrics. Whimsical animals made of ostrich eggs and enamel are displayed on the coffee table.

~ above ~

A charming painting of Persian odalisques floating over a city on cloudlike veils steals the show in this veranda masquerading as a dining room. Valentino lunches daily in his green-and-white striped tent. He chose an unusual centerpiece for the prettily set table—a large eighteenth-century Chinese lacquer pumpkin overflowing with small Brazilian silver fruits.

~ overleaf ~

The pool pavilion, with its mysterious voile-curtained openings and old Neopolitan-tiled walls, dazzles like a sultan's palace. Glamorous outdoor lighting metamorphoses it into a fantastic mirage afloat on the electric blue of the water. Umbrellas, commonly seen on Italian market stalls, shade a row of chaises. Baroque fish stand guard like aquatic sentinels.

FRANCO ZEFFIRELLI

1974

If anyone needs a retreat, it's Franco Zeffirelli, the esteemed director and set designer, who travels the world directing operas and making movies. His spiritual Eden—three small, white villas in the hills outside Positano, Italy—is surrounded by gardens and orchards, and linked by terraces and staircases. Flowers and sea commingle fragrantly to make "Tre Ville" as close to paradise as one can get. A keen gardener, Mr. Zeffirelli grows fruit trees, herbs, and vegetables abundant enough to feed his many and frequent guests. Indoors, the half-Moroccan villa exudes the exotic, with mirrored Indian fabrics and nineteenth-century Libyan furniture, a rhapsody of mother-of-pearl, ivory, and bleached wood. In Mr. Zeffirelli's tented bedroom, the checkerboard design of the Far Eastern fabric on the walls and ceiling is echoed in the straw rug.

~ above ~

A veranda shaded with a straw roof and fragrant with sweet-smelling flowers makes a perfect blind for boat and sea watching. Brightly printed Indian cotton cushions enliven the old-fashioned white wicker furniture.

~ left ~

Cool white prevails in the arched, tiled living room, an oasis from the hot summer sun. Tiny mirrors stud the white Indian cotton cloth that covers the banquettes and pillows. Two antique glass chandeliers flank an elaborately worked mirror. White lilies set off a bust of Maria Carolina, Queen of Naples.

DIANE VON FÜRSTENBERG

1976

No shrinking violet, Diane von Fürstenberg dares in whatever she does, whether it's going for broke with a glamorous pink-on-pink apartment; wearing to perfection the slinkiest, sexiest of jersey dresses; or building a fashion empire in a scant five years. Decorated by Robert Denning, her spacious New York apartment is a feminine fantasy, where she and her guests glow under pink lights and lounge around the dining table in commodious wing chairs. Mrs. von Fürstenberg reclines on a plump pink satin sofa that has been echoed in other permutations elsewhere in the apartment. Hanging above her is the de rigueur serial portrait by Andy Warhol.

~ above ~

When dining at the von Fürstenberg apartment, everybody gets the comfortable chairs, not just the lucky people at the head and the foot of the table. The subtle pink of the ceilings, picked up from the striped fabric upholstering the walls, continues into the living room beyond.

~ above ~

The entrance gallery becomes an extension of the living room, with the same yellow-and-peach geometric fabric on the walls, and identical slipcovers and cushions on the sofa and banquette. An ornate eighteenth-century Venetian marble-topped gilt table serves as a bar.

ROBERT MOTHERWELL

1977

Robert Motherwell chose to make an atelier of the ground floor of his barn in Greenwich, Connecticut, because of its expanse, high ceilings, and limited views. Here, he has ample room to spread out his collages, stack his paintings, and strew the floor with piles of his beloved art books. He appropriated the upstairs, where spatial high jinx take one's breath away, for fun—living, dining, reading, relaxing, and entertaining. In good country tradition, the living area combines old-fashioned white siding with a latticework of exposed beams. What furnishings there are—a mix of twentieth-century classics, simple antiques, and kilim rugs—give full play to the panoply of spectacular art.

PAINTING TECHNIQUE

~ above ~

Living over the studio has its architectural advantages: a geometry of exposed posts and beams, a gable library, and a vast skylight that suffuses the room with natural light. A cozy, informal lunch setting brings intimacy to the free-flowing largesse of the open space.

~ above ~

Like giant ribs, exposed wooden beams hold the space together. Bare parquet floors, white paneled walls, and a lack of clutter create an ideal ambience for showing off Motherwell's large canvases and Max Ernst's witty sculpture of a chess player.

ANN GETTY

1977

Only the breathtaking vista of the bay gives away the secret: this elegant neoclassical house is not located in London, as its English interior suggests, but in San Francisco. Ann Getty chose it for its grand scale and wonderful proportions, hallmarks of the architect Willis Polk, who designed it in 1913. She wanted spaces splendid enough to accommodate the most beautiful and individual eighteenth- and nineteenth-century English furniture she could find. In her spare time she treasure-hunted in the auction houses, galleries, and antique shops of London and New York. The bounty of that search—all museum-quality finds—resides harmoniously together, thanks to the judicious advice of the decorating firm of Parish-Hadley. A welcoming mood of festivity prevails with beautifully arranged flowers, candlelight, and chintz. Birds, a particular passion of Mrs. Getty's, stand guard on tables or fly about on screens, wall panels, porcelain, furniture, and upholstery.

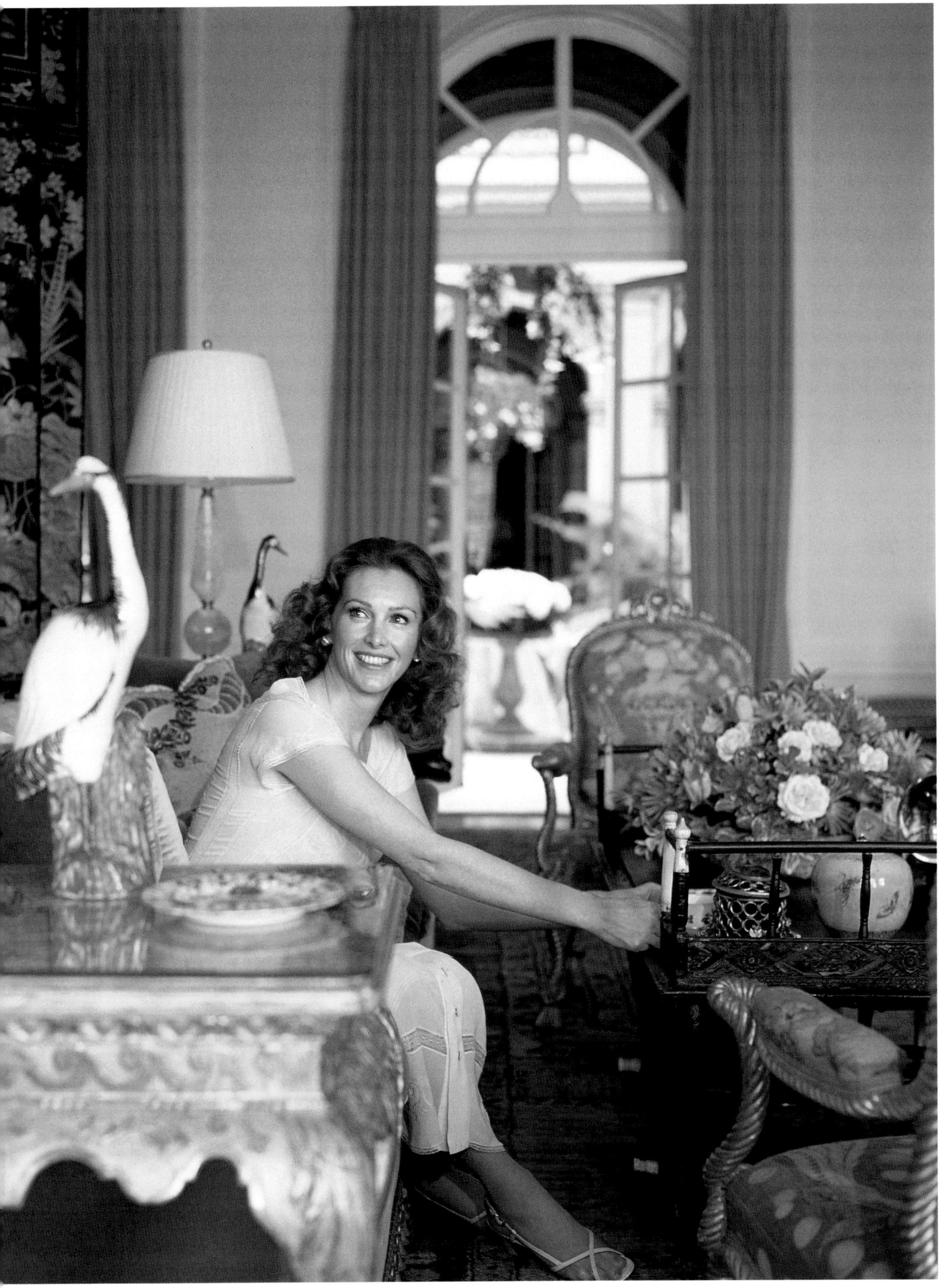

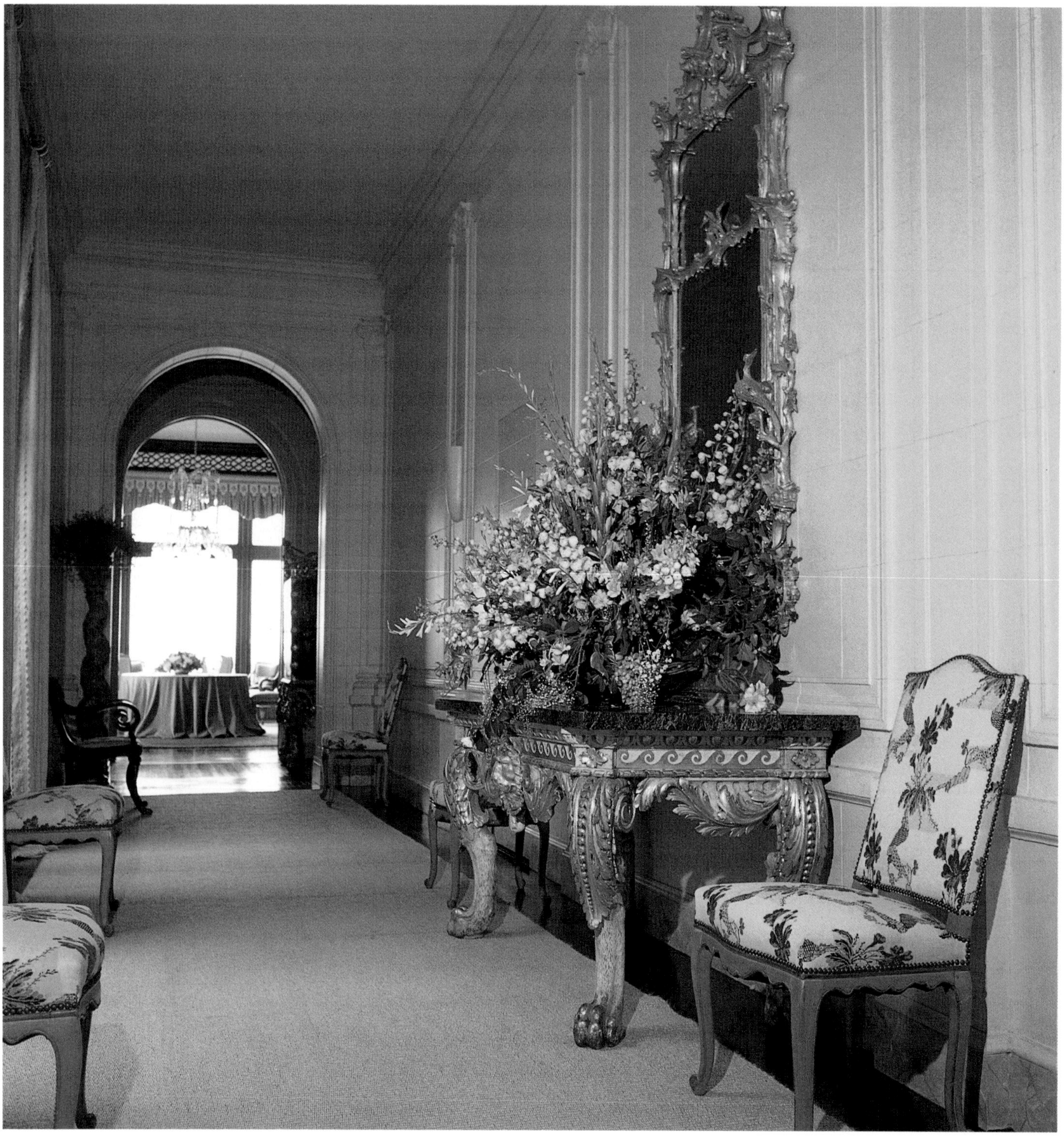

~ above ~

A long, grandly proportioned entrance hall is lined on both sides with fine eighteenth-century furniture. A ravishing flower arrangement is always on display to greet guests. Arched doors frame panoramic views of San Francisco Bay seen from the dining room.

~ above ~

In a dizzying array of crystal serpentines, a remarkable Russian chandelier illuminates the splendid dining room with candlelight. Eighteenth-century-style wall panels are bordered by mirrored treillage.

The sunny yellow of an English chintz sets the upbeat mood for this very pretty living room. A large Oriental rug ties the disparate furniture together. To the right of an exuberant rococo gilt mirror stands an imposing Chinese export cabinet.

DREDA MELE

1978

Agitation comes with the territory as director of a large fashion house in Paris, but on home ground Dreda Mele wants her surroundings to project the opposite. An envelope of whiteness brings calm to her ground-floor Paris apartment. The prevailing atmosphere of serenity is enhanced by furnishings spaced widely apart and French doors overlooking a large, shady garden. Miss Mele selected simple furniture and fabrics that live by their color. Exotic art and accessories collected on her frequent travels to the Orient are positioned so each stands out on its own. In the living room hot coral tones enliven eighteenth-century Burmese paintings, a pair of sofas, and a trio of Louis XV stools. An inlaid French bureau, a seventeenth-century red-lacquered Japanese screen, and an Italian hunting table displaying a golden Burmese Buddha mix compatibly despite differences in centuries and cultures.

At night Miss Mele illuminates her bathroom with the soft glow of candlelight. Large vases of pussy willow overhang a wonderfully commodious wood-paneled tub. Part of a collection of seashells, which she inherited from her grandmother, bedecks the corners of the tub. Comfort comes in the form of a gray-and-white geometric carpet and a velvet-covered armchair.

COUNTESS ISABELLE D'ORNANO

1978

La Renaudière is very much a family affair. Count Hubert d'Ornano inherited this eighteenth-century hunting lodge—on a five-thousand-acre estate south of Paris—from his uncle. The count commissioned his wife Isabelle's uncle, the Danish architect Mogens Twede, to transform it into a country house relaxed enough for five high-spirited children. The count then persuaded his wife to lend her considerable style and talents to the decoration of the interior. Countess d'Ornano, who has a strong sense of fantasy, came up with a charming scheme that mixes diverse prints, patterns, and colors with lavish bouquets of flowers, stunning antiques, and a plethora of comfortable sofas and chairs. Rest and relaxation are popular pastimes here. The old beams were left exposed to highlight the good bones of the structure and to enhance the warm, cozy atmosphere. The windows in the library were left uncurtained to let in maximum daylight; in other rooms sheer gauze curtains achieve the same end.

~ above ~

The library derives its warmth and feminine charm from a wall fabric in the manner of Odilon Redon. In witty contrast is a remarkable collection of nineteenth-century French engravings of Amazon women on horseback. A magnificent early Regency English table dominates the space.

~ above right ~

Dinners and hunt breakfasts are served in the wonderfully romantic winter garden sheltered in a glass-covered pavilion. Plates with animal scenes especially designed for La Renaudière bedeck the printed Porthault cloths. Painted, leather-covered Louis XVI chairs surround a large round table. A bevy of plants and a chandelier add to the atmosphere.

~ below right ~

The snugness of the master bedroom, sheltered under the eaves of the former attic, results from its felicitous architecture. A homey patchwork fabric on the bed, walls, and ceiling transforms the space into a seamless, cozy cocoon. A fanciful papier-mâché mirror found on the street in New York hangs above a handsomely tiled shelf for displaying objects and photos.

BARONESS MARIE-HÉLÈNE DE ROTHSCHILD

1978

After Baron Guy de Rothschild donated Ferrières, his nineteenth-century family chateau located outside Paris, to the University of Paris, he took up the challenge of building a smaller, contemporary house on the grounds. Baron Guy worked closely with architect Augustin Julia on every phase of the design and building of a new, shingled Ferrières in the Wrightian mode. The baron's wife, Marie-Hélène, masterminded the interior in collaboration with the designer François Catroux. Her goal was to distill the luxurious eclecticism of its illustrious namesake. The winter garden indicates how brilliantly she succeeded. A teak ceiling, recessed lights, and sheep by François Lalanne are pure twentieth century, but everything else bespeaks the splendor of a bygone era. Treasures from the seventeenth century include Venetian blackamoors, a sumptuous German cast-iron chest, and a German mirror on tooled Russian leather walls; finds from the nineteenth century comprise zany Victorian black leather love seats and chair with deep fringes.

~ above ~

A sophisticated piling on of rich pattern and color in the dining room contrasts charmingly with naive flowers that look like they were just cut in the garden. Batik cloths drape the tables; antique Indonesian shawls cover the banquettes and chairs. The delightful paneling, which could be an illustration for a children's book, was moved from the children's dining room at Sans Souci, another Rothschild chateau. Brilliantly colored eighteenth-century porcelain elephants from India carry candles on their backs.

~ above left ~

The naturalness of abundant plants and flowers in the living room leavens the luxury of precious objects and rich patterns. Another inspired bit of juxtapositioning: hanging a Reynolds portrait of Sarah Spencer Churchill and a hunting scene by Desportes on informal diamond-stenciled straw-covered walls. A Louis XIII Savonnerie tapestry turns the pouf into a center-stage perch of splendor.

~ below left ~

Airy yet exotic, this enchanting bedroom benefits from the beauty of the antique Indonesian shawls lavished on walls, curtains, and sleigh bed. Two compelling eighteenth-century Chinese paintings—a portrait of an empress and a landscape by a French missionary to China—add drama and focus. A curtained bathroom juts into the room and becomes part of it. Both a Louis XV bureau and the bed are angled for interest. The top of the unusual Brazilian palmwood night table is inlaid with butterflies.

A banquette upholstered in the same seventeenth-century Verdure tapestry that covers the floor invites relaxation in this splendid television room. On the walls behind, paintings by Desportes reiterate pastoral themes and colors in a vivid depiction of a wild boar hunt.

YVES SAINT LAURENT

1971 ~ 1983

The same artistry and originality that imbue the couture collections of Yves Saint Laurent permeate his duplex apartment in Paris and his Château Gabriel in Normandy. The chateau was decorated—in the spirit of Proust—by Jacques Grange. Whatever period or style Saint Laurent interprets, he garners the most exquisite artisanship in both architectural execu-

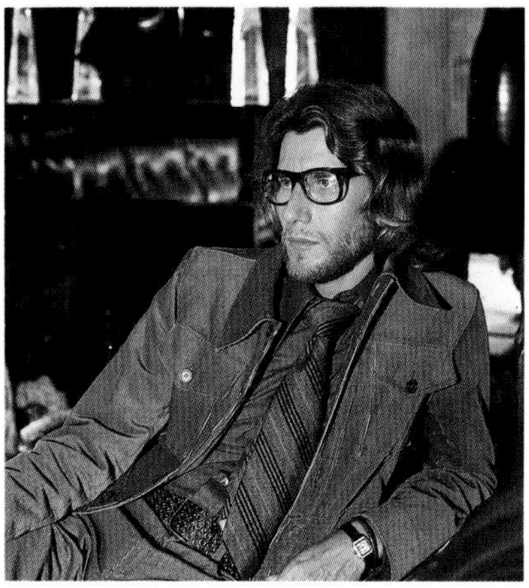

tion and furnishing. With the flair of his creative genius, he skillfully weaves together furniture, fabrics, art, and objects into a whole of incomparable luxury and uncommon interest. Saint Laurent's admiration for the 1930s is manifest in his Paris living room. Here, he wittily evokes the look of a grand salon on a glamorous French ocean liner—first class, of course! A portrait of Josephine Baker by Paul Colin—the painting was the model for the famous *Revue Nègre* poster—sets the proper art deco tone. Magnificent 1930s metal vases by Jean Dunand flank the fireplace.

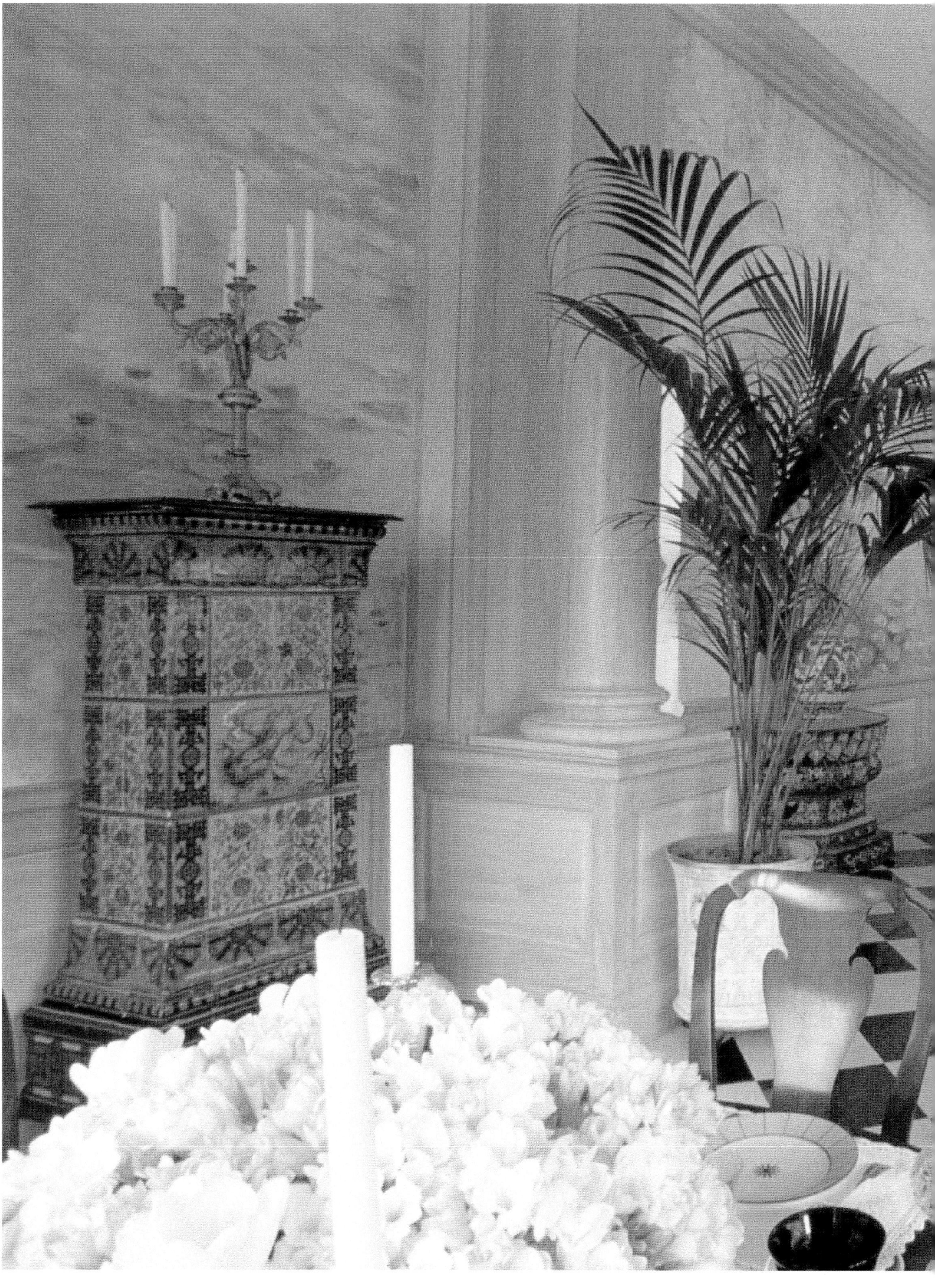

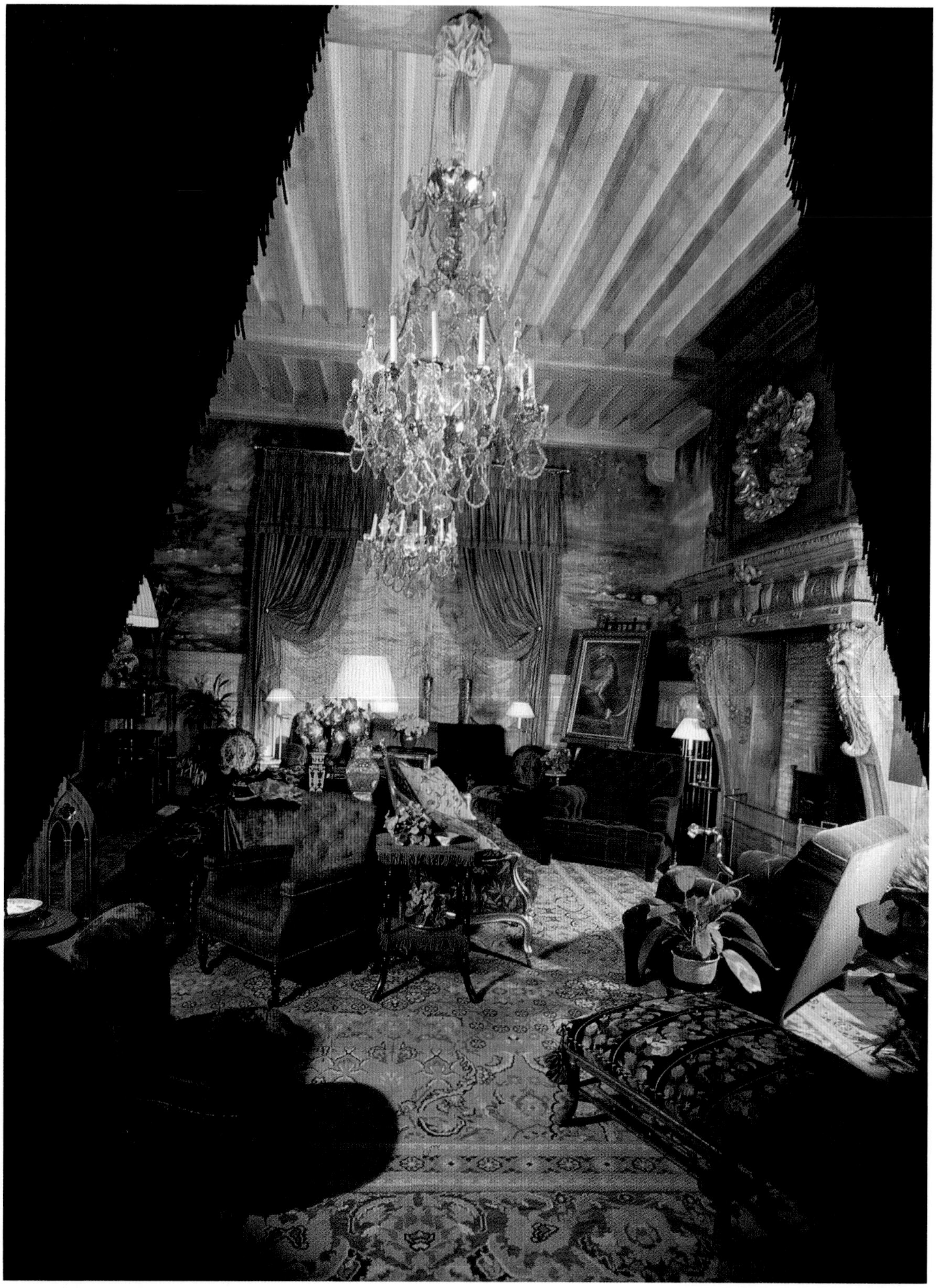

~ above ~

The opulent Second Empire salon is overwhelmingly grand—two crystal chandeliers, a baronial mantel, double-size velvet-covered armchairs, and wall murals of water lilies after Monet. A painting by Burne-Jones adds to the lushness.

~ preceding pages ~

In a regal dining room art, furniture, and objects compete in their splendor: on the walls are water lily murals painted in the style of Monet; at opposite ends spectacular Chinese pottery plinths display seventeenth-century ceramic vases. An exuberant nineteenth-century stove adds a colorful accent to the designated breakfast area.

~ above ~

In the center of the salon nature is rendered with high artifice and in exquisite detail: nineteenth-century silk-embroidered leaves burnish an antique velvet bench, a snake slithers across a ceramic leaf, and horses gallop around a cloisonné jar.

CANDICE BERGEN

1979

The duplex apartment of Candice Bergen is more about raw space than an abundance of rooms—it has only one bedroom off a second-floor balcony. Domesticating such a cavernous void is a problem many space-

hungry urban dwellers would adore to have. The young actress, aided by New York decorator Renny Saltzman, divided the enviable living area into the suggestion of rooms with furnishings that are comfortable, eclectic, and personal. Miss Bergen enjoys dazzling views of Central Park through a plethora of two-story windows. The seating compound is filled with mementos from her travels and keepsakes from her friends, such as the Chinese lamps given to her by Ali MacGraw. A nude by sculptor David Wynne reclines on a glass-and-rattan table. A Siamese Buddha makes an exotic counterpoint to an African carved wood-and-brass chest. Shots of color come from the kilim rugs, the pillows, and a classic Tiffany lamp.

When shutters close off the bedroom from the central living space, it becomes a cozy nest. A leather-topped mahogany partner's desk doubles as an office and a repository for such memorabilia as Miss Bergen's silver mug and baby rattles, and a spider paperweight given to her by Jack Nicholson. The raffia-frame, white duck headboard echoes the exuberant curve of the chair.

JOEL GREY & JO WILDER

1981

This Los Angeles cottage offers special charms, though not in the thatched roof, rambling roses style. Since busy lives, like the ones led by Joel Grey and Jo Wilder, are dominated by work and travel, less in a home means more freedom and easier upkeep. A compact, modern hideaway with light pink walls, bleached floors, and blue metal supports presents the ideal antidote to frantic schedules. A lack of clutter and a preponderance of flowers help create an atmosphere of light, air, and relaxed informality. Architect Franklin Israel designed an aerie for Mr. Grey which doubles as a study and a guest room, and tucked a cozy dining area underneath. The brick-paved patio, surrounded by a blossoming jungle of a garden provides a perfect haven for spending precious down time.

In the airy dining room an unlikely alliance of 1950s-style pottery from Woolworth, heavy Christofle silver, fine crystal, and white linen mats works splendidly. Artist Paul Fortune painted the canvas chair covers to look like pony skin.

ALEXANDER IOLAS

1981

Alexander Iolas, one of the great collectors of the century, commissioned his architect, Pikionis, to design a treasure trove. Fed up with paying huge sums for art storage, Iolas opted for a house in Athens large enough to warehouse art treasures from his galleries in New York, Paris, Milan, and Geneva. Pikionis obliged with a luxurious white marble palace so vast it easily accommodates a thousand cases of art bought all over the world. A perfectionist with a legendary eye, Iolas searched out the best—in art as well as furniture. He masterminded the decoration of the house, placing every treasure himself. The spectacular entrance portico is supported by massive antique columns with ram bases from Ravenna, Italy. Shimmering gold-sheathed doors decorated with warriors and centaurs were created by Pikionis.

~ left ~

An upstairs salon with wall-to-wall art feels more like a museum than a sitting room. Against the left wall is a *Nanas* sculpture by Niki de Saint Phalle and a painting by Fontana. A large mural by Harold Stevenson decorates the back wall. In the center of the room are Magritte's amusing bird cage chair and a jumble of concrete books by Eliseo Mattiacci.

~ preceding pages ~

The center-stage star of this elaborate French Empire guest room is one of Mr. Iolas's favorite works, a very pure, very fine Greek marble sculpture of Aesculapius. Two finely embroidered Greek area rugs contrast simply with a flood of gold satin in upholstery and draperies, and a profusion of ormolu mounts. A wonderful variety of candelabra embellishes the room and softly lights it.

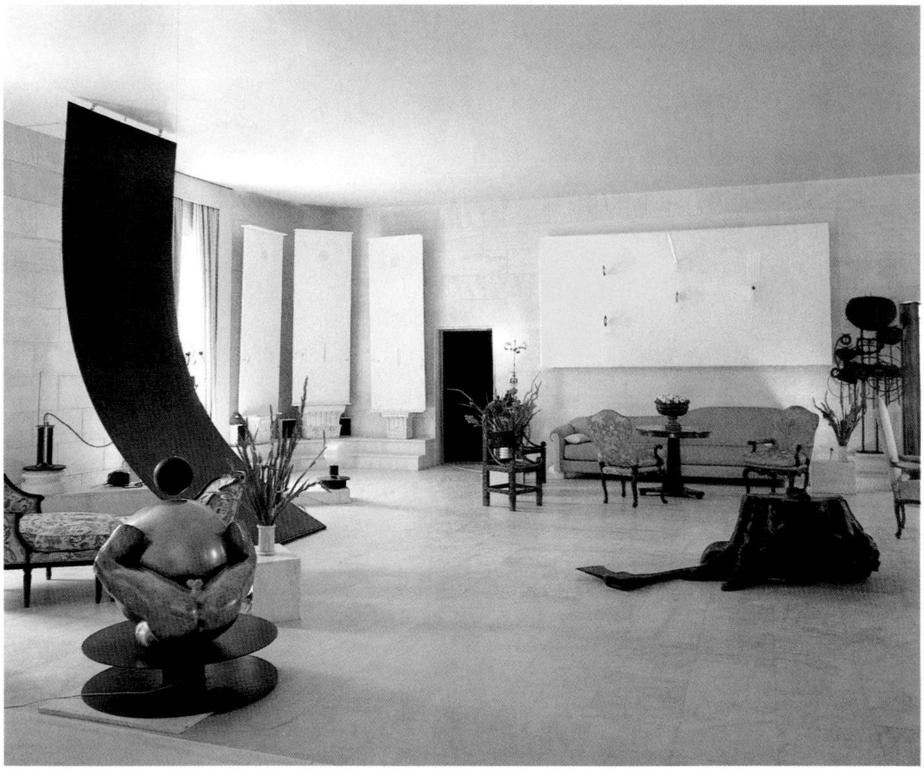

~ above ~

The palatially scaled upstairs salon, with its vast expanse of white marble, easily accommodates such large works by Takis as a black metal slide and suspended ball, three white paintings mounted on stone capitals, and a three-dimensional yellow painting.

~ left ~

On one of many white marble terraces around the house, two works by Takis are prominently displayed: an erotic sculpture in the foreground and a giant iron flower in the corner. Large white marble spheres tossed randomly on the floor look like oversize boccie balls.

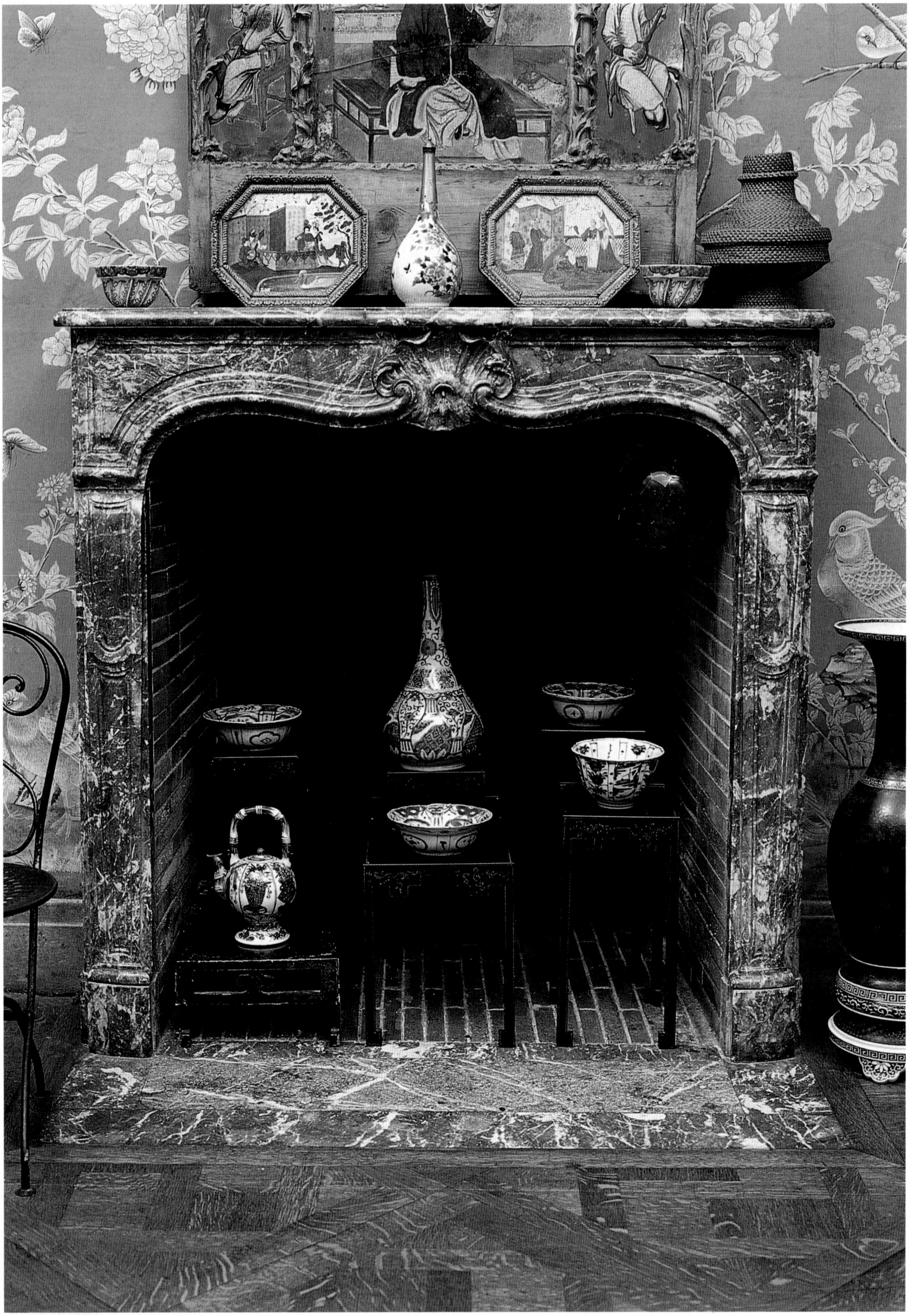

BARON PHILIPPE DE ROTHSCHILD

1982

Baron Philippe de Rothschild, the writer, translator, winemaker, and eccentric in a family of internationally famous bankers, lives in the small eighteenth-century Paris house that was home to his late wife, Pauline. The baroness, who was American, lived in the house both before and after her marriage. ("Philippe Baron Philippe," as he likes to be called, resided separately, in a much larger duplex apartment across town.) A passionate admirer of his wife's exquisite taste and eye for quality, he made only slight changes in the interior: a new canopy on a steel-framed bed she designed and the addition of a sketch of Mlle de Provence, Louis XV's daughter. Philippe Baron Philippe relishes the tranquil country-house atmosphere the garden inspires. In the *salon vert* the luminous green of a hand-painted eighteenth-century Chinese wallpaper makes a perfect counterpoint to the baroness's extraordinary collection of blue-and-white ceramics.

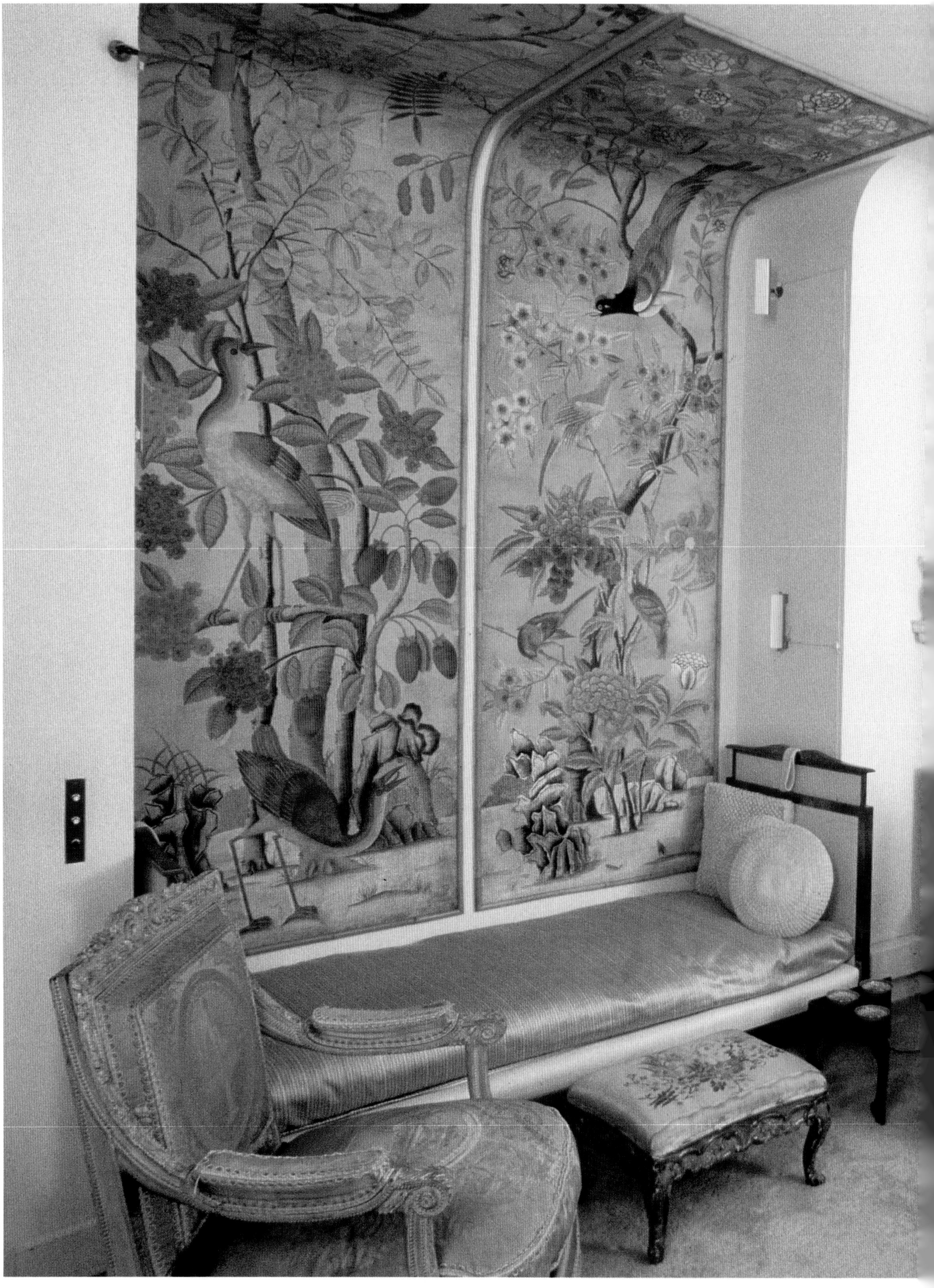

~ above ~

The only whimsy in this austere bedroom can be found on the walls: cartoon-like scenes cut from antique Chinese wallpaper and framed in bamboo and rattan, are hung en masse. Designed by Pauline de Rothschild, the unique bed consists of steel rods calibrated by brass rings and topped with a simple, tailored canopy.

~ right ~

Though small, the oval salon is packed with exquisite furniture. An English Regency mirror with a chinoiserie panel hangs above a Louis XVI settee. Charles X chairs surround a portable table that "Philippe Baron Philippe" has set wherever he feels like eating. The silk twist at the window is Pauline de Rothschild's adaption from an eighteenth-century painting.

~ preceding pages ~

Baldachins created out of exuberant, hand-painted eighteenth-century Chinese wallpaper panels transform the low ceilings of this room into assets. A magnificent commode ornamented with bronze-doré mounts displays Pauline de Rothschild's rare Chinese porcelains. Louis XVI chairs covered in their original silk flank a steel-framed daybed designed by the baroness.

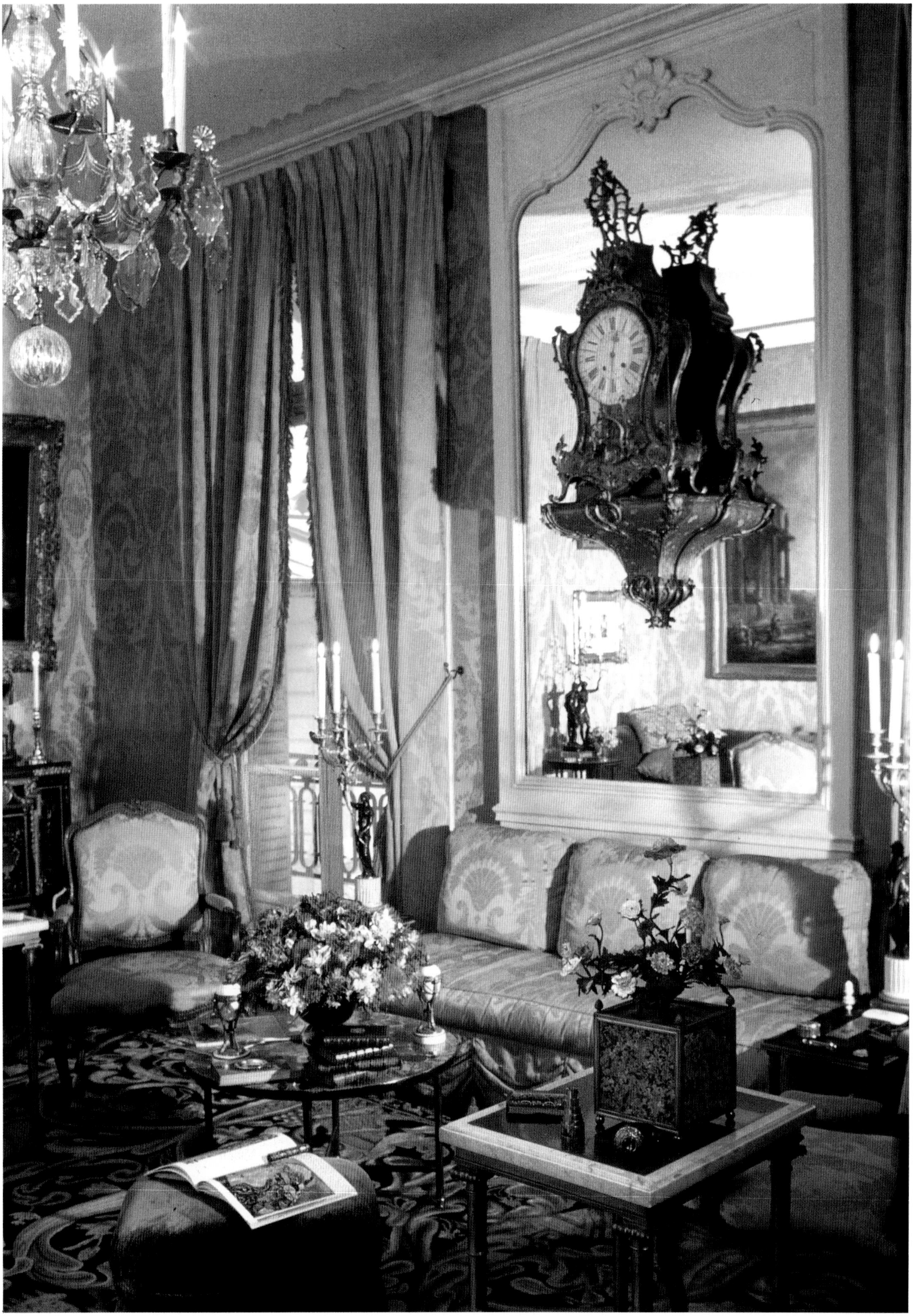

VICOMTESSE JACQUELINE DE RIBES

1984

Though miles of road and expectations about town and country separate the Paris house and the rural estate of Vicomtesse Jacqueline de Ribes, high style links the two. Wonderfully civilized, they share certain hallmarks: monumentally scaled rooms, handsome French antique furniture, lots of precious objects, a generous display of glorious flowers, and strong, clear, regal colors. Their differences involve the trappings of formality: in Paris yards and yards of silk, crystal chandeliers, and French tapestry rugs; and in the country a bounty of cotton Oriental carpets, cashmere throws, and petit-point upholstery. Tradition holds sway in each residence. Here, Vicomtesse de Ribes descends the breathtakingly beautiful spiral staircase of her country house. Behind her hangs a historic collection of faience plates made in secret in praise of the monarchy during the French Revolution. In the salon of her majestic Paris house, marigold yellow brocade sets off a magnificent antique French clock hung in front of a tall, dramatic mirror.

~ above ~

In Paris, at large dinner parties, round tables spill over into a magnificent gallery hung with eighteenth-century Beauvais tapestries. Pristine white tablecloths focus full attention on a delightful centerpiece of candles and old-fashioned flowers.

~ right ~

In an urbane country house, dark green walls and mirror-polished parquet floors compose a formal background for Louis XVI chairs, Oriental rugs, porcelain snuff boxes, and vases overflowing with flowers. Cashmere throws and touches of old lace prettily warm up the drawing room.

Flanking the fireplace, the enormous windows in the drawing room are hung with a royal pairing of lace curtains and red cotton draperies edged with gold. A de Ribes family portrait hangs above an important Régence commode.

PALOMA PICASSO

1985

If there's truth in the adage "people look like their places," Paloma Picasso affirms it in her Manhattan duplex. With her ebony hair, alabaster skin, and signature red lips, she embodies the drama of the black-and-white interior, which serves as a striking background for a unique collection of her father's art. The same quality, flair, and fine workmanship that distinguish the jewelry Paloma designs for Tiffany is exhibited on a grander scale in her apartment, which she decorated with her husband, Rafael Lopez-Sanchez, a playwright and a director. Given the glamorous 1930s look of the apartment, with its abundance of show-stopping art deco furniture, is it surprising that Paloma wanted to play the movie role of Coco Chanel, who defined 1930s style?

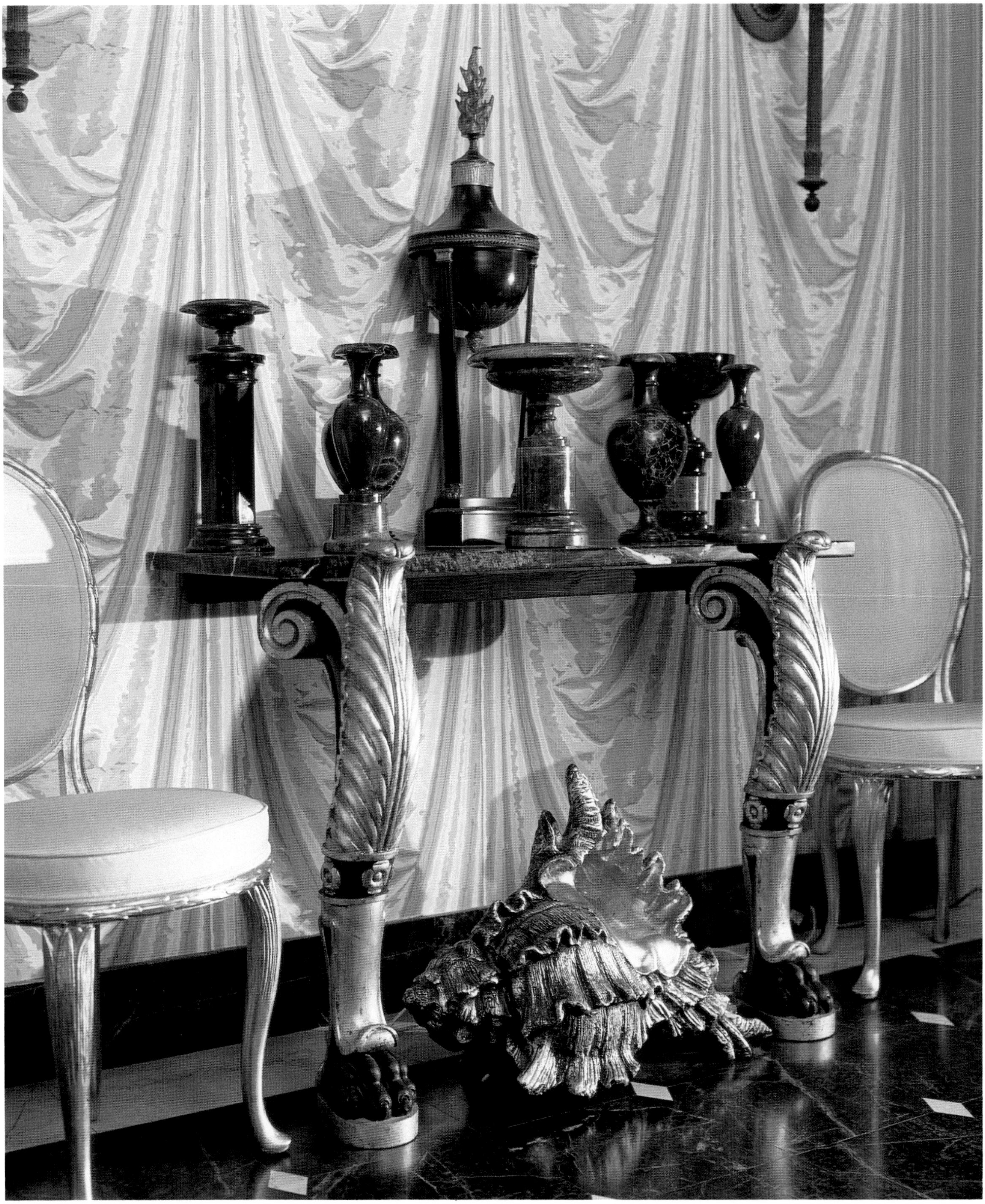

~ above ~

Front and center in a dramatic entry hall is this sophisticated still life, played out against a gray-and-white trompe l'oeil of draped silk. Delicate art deco chairs by Jules Leleu flank an imposing console with huge paw feet which displays a varied collection of serpentine nineteenth-century vases.

~ above and below ~

In the living room an inspired juxtaposing of torsos and heads: two by Picasso, his 1937 painting *Woman with a Vase of Holly* and the 1950 bronze *Pregnant Woman,* and two antiquities, a stucco head and an Egyptian statuette of the falcon deity. In her study Paloma accented the playfulness of a nineteenth-century swinging daybed with a wanton purple velvet cover. A mirror with figured supports and a bronze sphinx top a draped table.

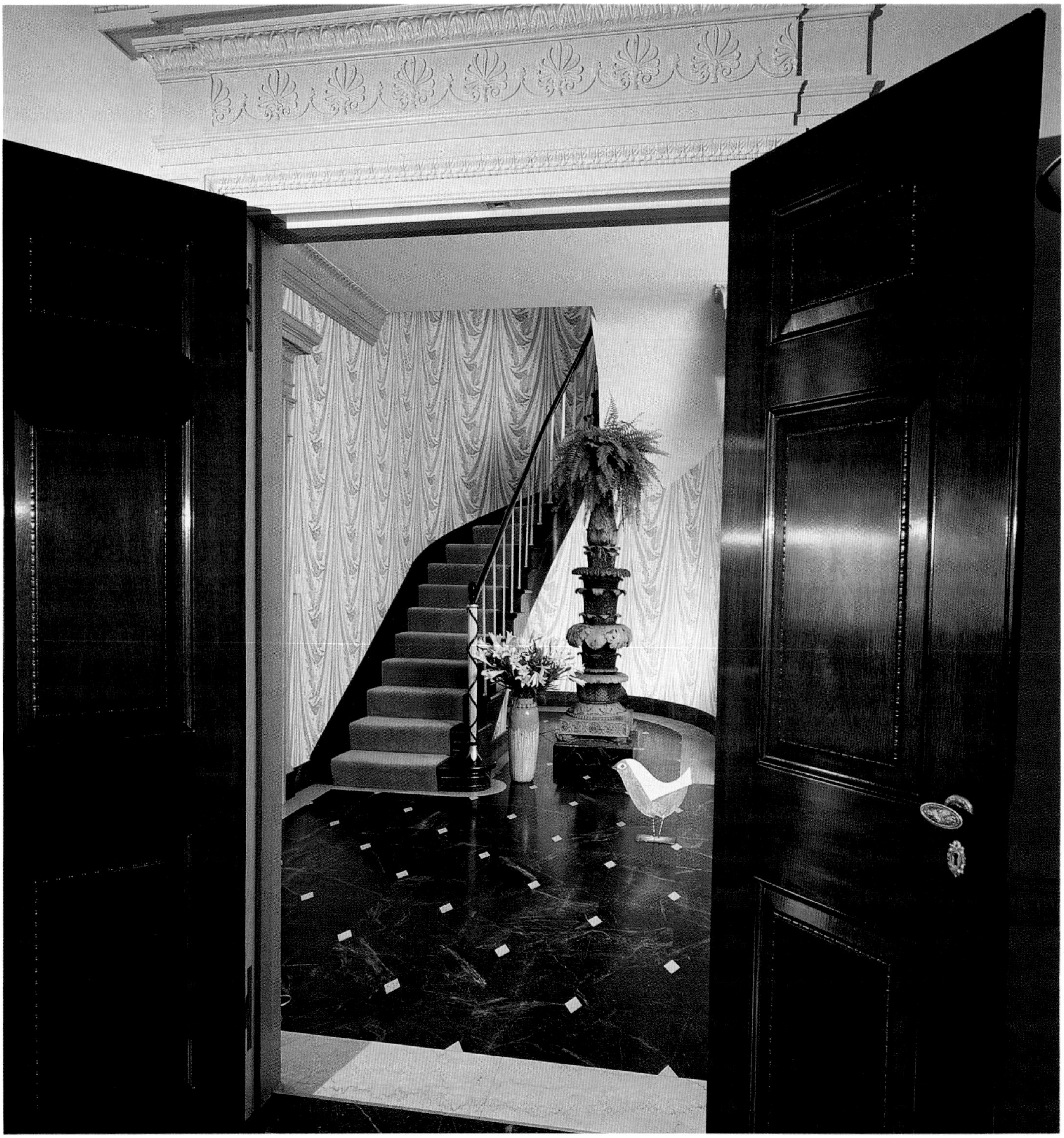

~ above ~

Highly polished mahogany doors make a warm background for the cool green marble floor and grisaille walls of the entry hall. A witty ensemble of an eccentric bronze Victorian plant stand, a bird sculpture, and an attenuated green vase hint at treasures to come. Neoclassical detailing on the stair baluster introduces a dominant theme of the apartment.

~ preceding pages ~

The kick-up-your-heels orange of silk taffeta draperies takes the edge off the formality of the gold, black, and white scheme in this splendid living room. A stunning medallioned nineteenth-century Bessarabian carpet both keys the color scheme and anchors the black lacquer seating group. A gilded tin roof ornament in the center of the coffee table looks like a precious art object. Eighteenth-century Venetian lions and carved marble columns frame the neoclassical mantel.

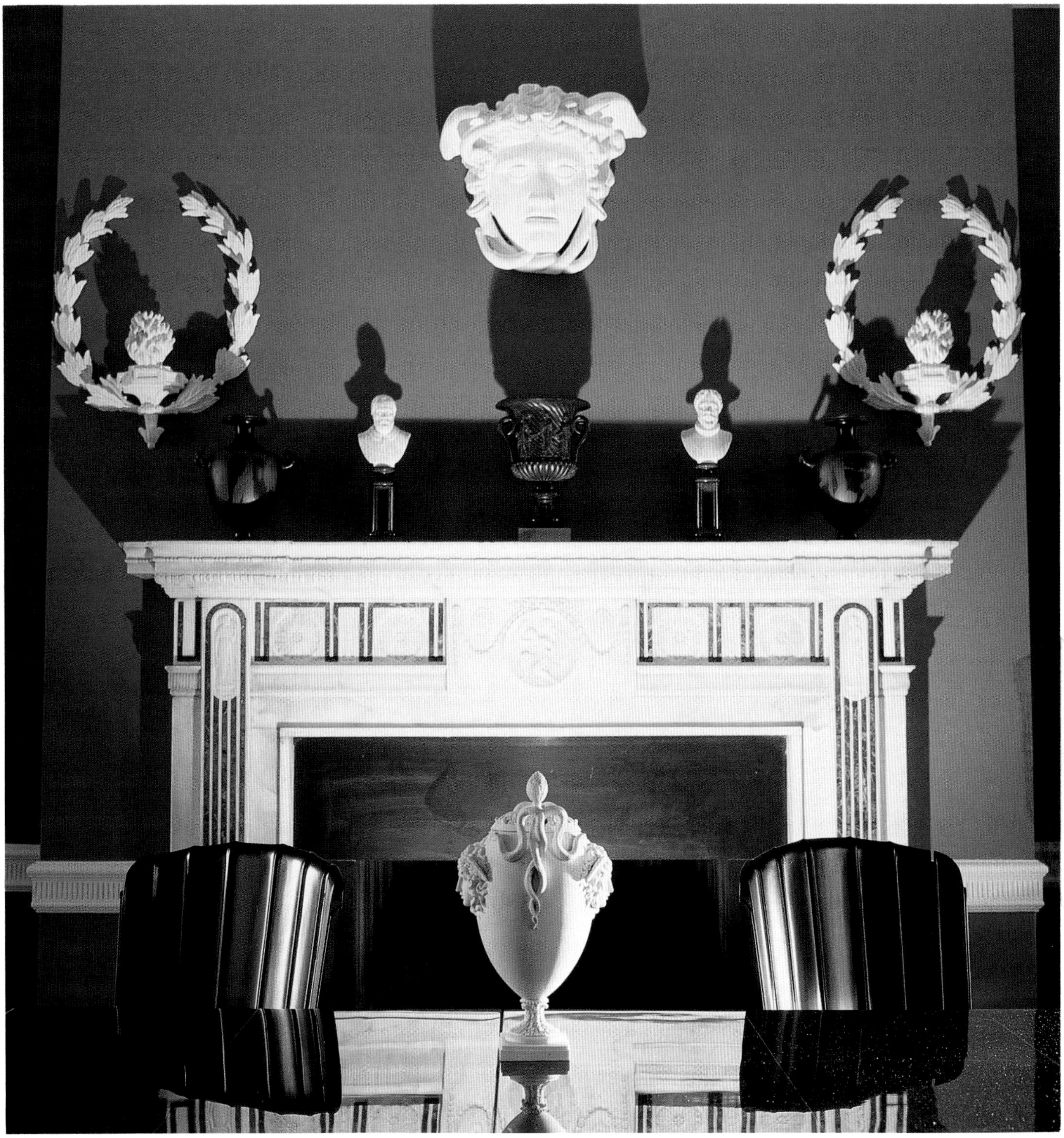

~ above ~

A mirror finish on the black lacquer dining table is so perfect it reflects the white marble mantel etched with green marble and the shiny black art deco chairs by Emile-Jacques Ruhlmann. Arrayed in strict neoclassical symmetry on the mantel, against a vivid blue-green wall, are marble busts of Galileo and Tasso, and vases painted in the Etruscan style.

LINDA TAUBMAN

1986

The spare, lean ethos of modernism has been laid like a template over the charming eclectic jumble that fills this large, comfortable house near Detroit. Linda Taubman—whose husband, Robert, is an executive with the Taubman Company, banished busyness from her rooms in favor of breezy openness. With the help of decorator William Hodgins, she indulged her passion for white, restricting pattern to art and Oriental rugs. The serenely monochromatic scheme brings strong focus to Mrs. Taubman's special collecting interests: antique chairs and tables that are so strong in line, proportion, and detail they function in the space like sculptures. In the study a painting of an odalisque by Douglas Joseph, vintage 1921, reigns supreme. An Italian neoclassical chair, circa 1830, and a giddily exuberant rococo table play off the exoticism of the radiant painting.

~ above ~

As an antidote to their peripatetic lives, the Taubmans wanted their bedroom to be a tranquil cocoon where they could wind down. They also wanted it to double as a second living room. A calming blanket of white brings all the disparate elements together. The windows, with simple shades, defer to the drama of the elaborately curtained bed.

~ above right ~

The shell-like curve of a staircase endows this elegant foyer with a timeless grace. Free-flowing space and the aureole of daylight streaming through a high bay window enhance a spare but perfect collection of treasures: an eighteenth-century table with gilt swan legs, a classic bust of Voltaire, and a wonderfully proportioned Regency chair.

~ below right ~

The light, airy, and intentionally low-key living room plays a supporting role to the wonders of nature on display in the Taubman's splendid garden, seen through the French windows. The furniture, grouped on an Oriental rug and scattered strategically on a bare bleached floor, provides the room with an uncluttered look. A subtle blue velvet on the Louis XVI chairs adds the barest dash of color.

PATRICIA KLUGE

1988

It would be hard to imagine packing more glamour, more art, more luxury, more marble, and more awe-inspiring space into this New York pied-à-terre belonging to Patricia and John Kluge. Mr. Kluge, who owns and runs Metromedia, Inc., the broadcast giant, takes an elevator to work, since his apartment is right in the Metromedia building. The design was envisioned by Mrs. Kluge, who stands next to a Salvador Dalí sculpture: For her, the design had to represent high energy and the future, and had to reflect Metromedia, the Kluges' style, and New York City. She wanted to take elements from nature, such as trees, and bring them indoors. Designers Richard Ohrbach and Lynn Jacobson gave form to her fantasy. In the foyer, a sweeping staircase sets the stage for Robert Graham's drama of nudes, a single bronze sculpture and a frieze beneath the banister. The color extravaganza on the wall behind is a billboard-sized painting by Frank Stella.

FRANK STELLA

Great marble columns hold a Botero triptych aloft
like a proud banner of corpulence. A veritable galaxy of
spotlights tinted peach and pink bounce, shimmer, and
shine off polished marble floors and a burnished gold ceiling.
The purpose of this "everything room?" Entertaining.

LADY CAROLINE SOMERSET

1983

David Somerset and his wife, Lady Caroline, who stands in the book-lined library near a table covered with a quilt she made by hand, have the great good fortune to live in "The Cottage." It might well be everyone's dream of an English country house—blazing fires, omnipresent chintz, fine antiques, generous flower arrangements, beautiful rugs, and faithful dogs. And exceptional gardens. With the help of famed landscape architect Russell Page, they designed the gardens as rooms walled with hedges of yew, holly, and Portuguese laurel thronged with old-fashioned roses. What's more, the Somersets are fortunate in being able to visit neighboring Badminton, one of the great English baronial estates, whenever they like. The country seat of the Beaufort family, Badminton was built in 1682 and enlarged by William Kent in 1750. The public can visit only on specified days, but the Somersets can pop by whenever they like because David Somerset is the Duke of Beaufort's cousin and future heir.

~ above ~

A library with welcoming ways: a crackling fire in the fireplace is augmented by a butler's table literally heaped with flowers. Thirty-seven small vases of various sorts are filled with violets, pansies, phlox, green foxglove, lavender, marjoram, dill, verbena, and tobacco. Magazines are piled casually on needlepoint stools stitched by Lady Caroline.

~ right ~

Filled with caps, hunting hats, walking sticks, and mackintoshes, the vivacious front hall suggests the energetic life of the house. Pervasive flowers—stitched in needlepoint on chair coverings, painted on porcelain bowls, stacked on the floor, and overflowing from a basket—offset an aura of quotidian practicality, as do the landscapes and seascapes framing a gilt mirror.

BRISTOL.

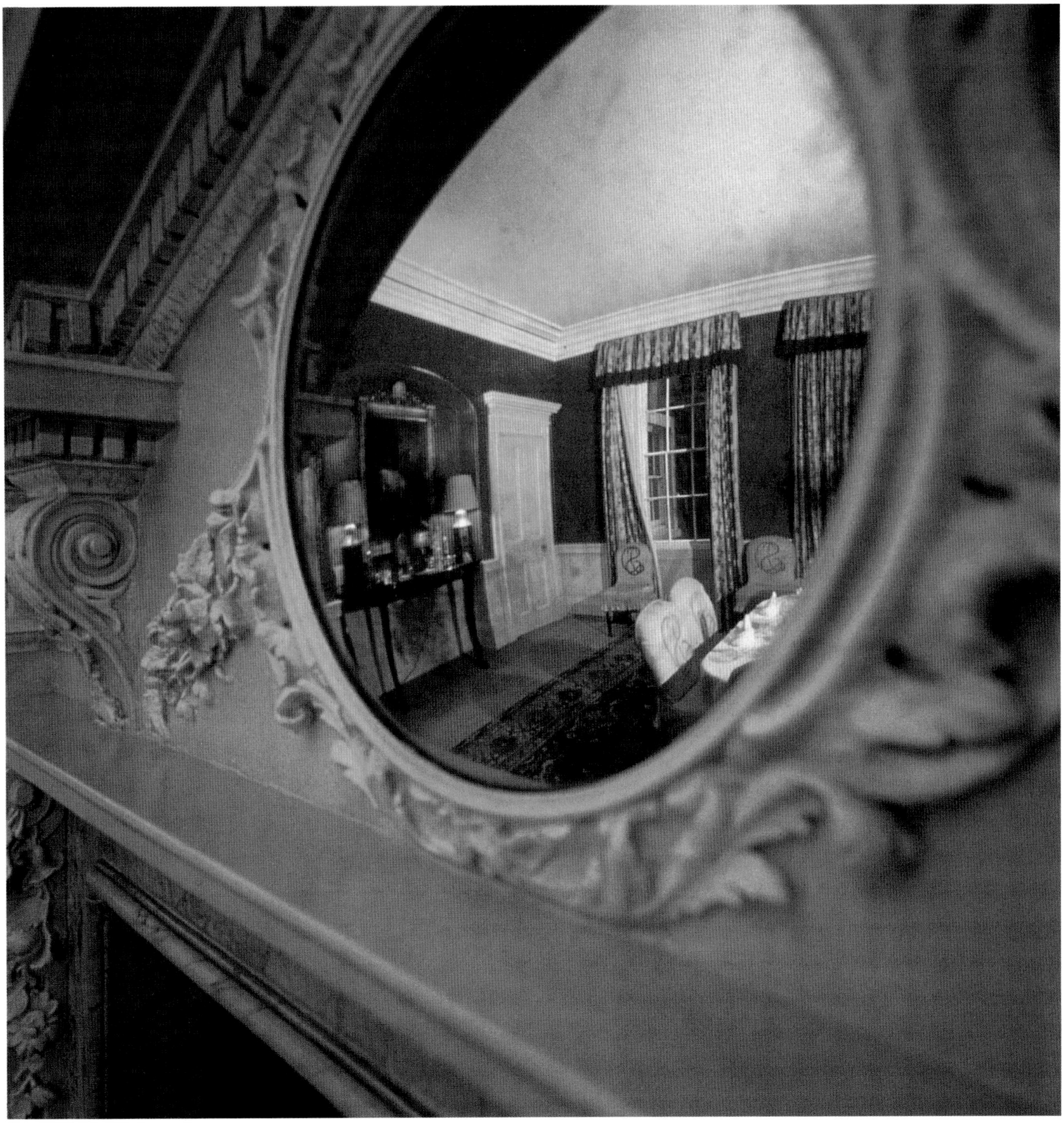

~ above ~

A mirror framed by elaborate plasterwork on the overmantel reflects the red dining room decorated by Tom Parr. Lady Caroline echoed the red of the lacquer walls in initials she outlined in needlepoint on white linen slipcovers. A horse painting in a frame designed by William Kent hangs in a niche.

~ above left ~

In an extra sitting room, known as "The Men's Room"—brandy and cigars, anyone?—appropriately beat-up, leather club chairs flank the fireplace. Favorite pictures from a book illustrated by Claude Lorrain cover the walls.

~ below left ~

In the stable sumptuously caparisoned harnesses for driving horses make engaging counterpoints to the graphic simplicity of a no-nonsense Bristol clock.

ANDY WARHOL

1983

Andy Warhol is a legend in his own time, not just for his celebrated pop paintings but also for the life-style he orchestrated in his self-proclaimed "Factory." Within its stark, white-walled shell, his vintage 1870s warehouse accommodates a loftlike studio, where Mr. Warhol paints portraits of the beautiful people (among other things); the "boardroom" where he entertains them; the offices of *Interview* magazine, which he founded; and a vast, eclectic collection of antiques he can't resist adding to. In the wood-paneled boardroom Mr. Warhol serves his famous "cold cuts" luncheon from an Irish Regency sideboard. Behind him hangs a large, melancholy painting by Scottish Pre-Raphaelite David Forrester Wilson.

~ above ~

In the boardroom carved East African sculptures frame a moosehead that looks right at home on the dark paneled walls. Emile-Jacques Ruhlmann designed the elegantly detailed chairs and conference table disguised by a slate top put on for protection.

~ above ~

In his studio Mr. Warhol casually mixes his paintings with French finds: an art moderne overhead fixture from the Paris flea market and an exquisite art deco brass desk.

TERRY STANFILL

1985

Anyone who has had a love affair with Italy—and who hasn't?—will be totally bewitched by the southern California house of Terry Stanfill. An activist for Save Venice and a collector, she has created an interior that is as much fun to browse in as a splendid art book. In the lively, airy dining room-cum-library, a pavilion-like gilt wood eighteenth-century birdcage masquerades as a chandelier. The lighting, soft and romantic, actually emanates from an early-nineteenth-century candelabrum on a Baccarat base. In front of the French doors, Neopolitan candlesticks shaped like reclining muses flank a Temple of Love that enshrines a Hellenistic marble figure of Aphrodite. The table is exquisitely set with nineteenth-century Russian plates and Saint Petersburg flatware with handles of *pietra dura* and porcelain. An extraordinary painting from Bologna, circa 1627, hangs over the fireplace.

~ above right ~

A tapestry top on a Régence table provides a rich and colorful backdrop for displaying favorite collections — boxes and blue-and-white pottery. Elaborate gilt mirrors from Piedmont flank an eighteenth-century painting of Venice by William James. An intricate maquette for a Venetian garden resides on an antique English table.

~ below right ~

In the loggia Mrs. Stanfill has contrived an inspired arrangement of a magnificent eighteenth-century Neopolitan screen, Roman chairs covered in blue Fortuny silk, blue-and-white Chinese vases, and a Genoese bench with a gilt base. Along the wall a Korean lacquer Burgauté chest shows off more blue and white.

~ above ~

A pair of French hand puppets and a Genoese crèche make charming and lighthearted counterpoints to a regal eighteenth-century Neopolitan bed. The exuberantly painted headboard depicts a phoenix glorified by a joyous array of colorful flowers.

~ above ~

Playing off the colors and patterns of a Gobelins fragment against those of an Aubusson rug creates a compelling visual synergy in the living room. The angelic remnant on the eighteenth-century taboret was part of a tapestry made for a ceiling.